A QUICK COURSE IN

EXCEL 4

For Windows

JOYCE COX

PATRICK KERVRAN

PUBLISHED BY
Online Press Incorporated
14320 NE 21st Street, Suite 18
Bellevue, WA 98007
(206) 641-3434
(800) 854-3344

Publisher's Cataloging in Publication
(prepared by Quality Books Inc.)

Cox, Joyce, 1946–
  A quick course in Excel 4 for windows / Joyce K. Cox, Patrick Kervran.
    p. cm.
    Includes index.
    ISBN 1-879399-15-6

    1. Windows (Computer programs) 2. Electronic spreadsheets (Computer programs)   I. Kervran, Patrick.   II. Title.   III. Title: Excel 4 for windows.

QA76.76.W56C6 1992   005.4'3
                                       QBI92-122
                                       92-60031
                                              CIP

Printed and bound in the United States of America

1 2 3 4 5 6 7 8 9 X Y A L 3 2 1 0

Distributed to bookstores by Publishers Group West, (800) 788-3123

Contents

1

Building a Simple Worksheet

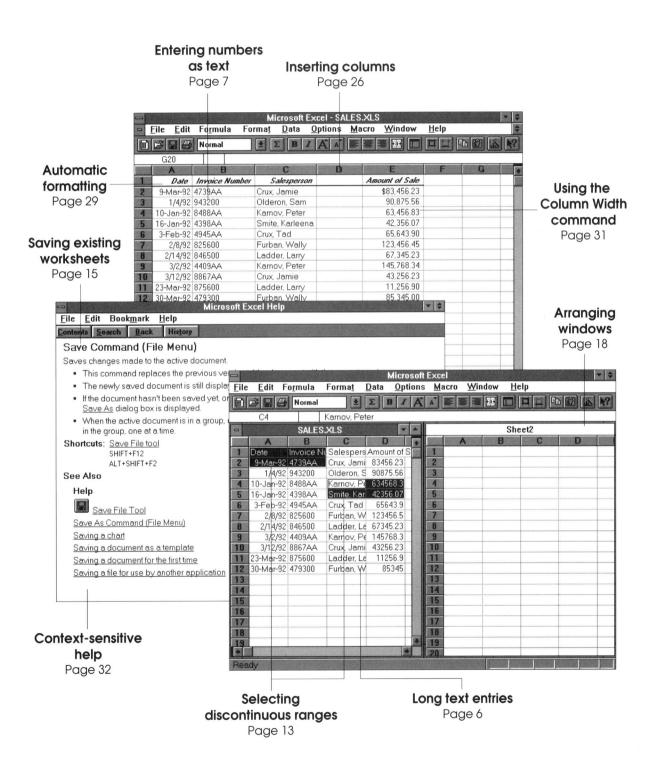

Entering numbers
as text
Page 7

Inserting columns
Page 26

Automatic
formatting
Page 29

Using the
Column Width
command
Page 31

Saving existing
worksheets
Page 15

Arranging
windows
Page 18

Context-sensitive
help
Page 32

Selecting
discontinuous ranges
Page 13

Long text entries
Page 6

You're probably sitting at your computer, anxious to start crunching numbers. But before we get going, we need to cover some basics, such as how to enter text and numbers, save files, move around a worksheet, edit and format entries, and print the results of your labors. After we discuss a few fundamentals, you'll easily be able to create the worksheets and charts we cover in the rest of the book.

We assume that you've already installed Windows 3.0 or a later version and Excel 4 on your computer. We also assume that you've worked with Windows before and that you know how to start programs, move windows, choose commands from menus, highlight text, and so on. If you are a Windows novice, we recommend that you take a look at *A Quick Course in Windows*, another book in the Quick Course series, which will help you quickly come up to speed.

To follow the instructions in this book, you should be using a mouse. Although it is theoretically possible to work in Windows and Excel using just the keyboard, we would not wish that fate on anyone, and most of our instructions involve using a mouse. Occasionally, however, when it is easier or faster to use the keyboard, we give the keyboard equivalent of the mouse action.

Well, let's get going. With the DOS prompt (C:>) on your screen, start Windows by typing *win* and pressing Enter. Then,

Other ways of starting

To start Excel (or any other Windows program) directly from the DOS prompt, type *win*, a space, and the name of the program. For Excel, type *win excel* and press Enter. Windows locates Excel, bypassing the Windows Program Manager. You can also start Excel with a document already loaded by typing *win excel*, a space, and the name of the document.

Worksheet icons

You can create icons for frequently used worksheets that will be displayed in Program Manager. Simply make a copy of the Microsoft Excel icon, and choose the Properties command from Program Manager's File menu. Then change the Command Line text box to include the name of the worksheet you want to represent with the icon, and click OK.

Missing Excel group?

The Excel installation program creates the Microsoft Excel 4.0 group by default. If you do not have a Microsoft Excel 4.0 group, someone might have moved Excel to a different group and deleted the Excel group. Open the other group windows (Windows Applications is a likely candidate), locate the Microsoft Excel icon, and double-click it to start the program.

in Windows, start Excel by double-clicking the Microsoft Excel icon in the Microsoft Excel 4.0 group window.

Starting Excel

Getting Oriented

When you start Excel for the first time, your screen looks something like this:

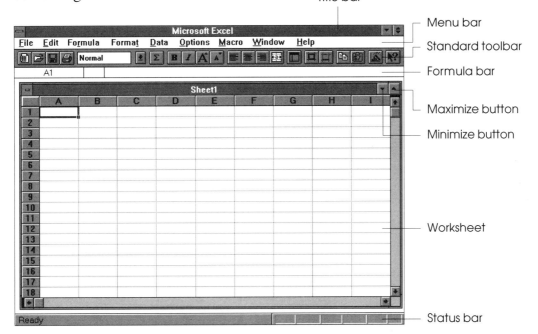

Title bar

Menu bar

Standard toolbar

Formula bar

Maximize button

Minimize button

Worksheet

Status bar

At the top of the screen is the Microsoft Excel title bar, followed by the menu bar, from which you choose commands. Below the menu bar is the Standard toolbar, an Excel feature that puts a host of often-used tools within easy reach. (The Standard toolbar is one of nine toolbars available in Excel.) Below the Standard toolbar is the formula bar, in which you enter the values (text and numbers) and formulas that you'll use in your worksheet.

Taking up the majority of the screen is the blank worksheet, which as you can see, is laid out in a grid of columns and rows like the ledger paper used by accountants. The rectangle at the junction of each column and row is called a cell. Each cell has a reference that consists of the letter displayed in the heading at the top of the cell's column and the number displayed in the heading at the left end of its row. For example, the reference of the cell in the top-left corner of the worksheet, which is always active when you start Excel with

Cell references

a blank worksheet, is A1. The reference of the cell below A1 is A2, and the reference of the cell to the right of A1 is B1. Excel displays the reference of the active cell—the one you are currently working with—at the left end of the formula bar.

The worksheet has 256 columns, lettered A through IV, and 16,384 rows, numbered 1 through 16384, for a total of over 4 million cells. Potentially, you could create a worksheet 20 feet wide by 80 feet long—large enough for just about any set of calculations, short of the national budget.

At the bottom of the screen is the status bar, which displays useful information about menu and tool selections and about the status of keys, such as whether Num Lock or Caps Lock is turned on.

Entering Text

Most spreadsheets consist of blocks of text and numbers in table format on which you can perform various calculations. To make the tables easy to decipher, you usually give the columns and rows labels that describe their associated entries. Let's try entering a few labels now:

Entering headings

1. With cell A1 selected on the blank worksheet, type *Date*. Cell A1 is the active cell, meaning that anything you type will appear there. As you type, the text is displayed in both the formula bar and the cell. In the formula bar, an insertion point

The status bar and toolbar

If you don't see the status bar or the toolbar, choose the Workspace command from the Options menu, select Status Bar, and click OK. To display the Standard toolbar, choose Toolbars from the Options menu, select Standard, and click Show. (For information about how to choose commands from menus, see page 13.)

Mouse pointer shapes

The mouse pointer takes on different shapes depending on where it is on the screen. For example, the pointer is a cross when it is over the worksheet; an arrow when it is over a menu command, the toolbar, or the title bar; a double-headed arrow when it is over a column or row heading border; and a text tool (or I-beam) when it is over the formula bar.

Selected cells

When you open an existing Excel worksheet, the cells that were selected when you closed the worksheet are still selected. This is a good indicator of where you were last working in the worksheet.

leads the way, telling you where the next character you type will be inserted. The Enter box and the Cancel box also appear in the formula bar. Meanwhile, the indicator in the status bar changes from *Ready* to *Enter*, because the text you have typed will not be recorded in cell A1 until you "enter" it.

2. One way to record the entry is to click the Enter box—the box with a check mark in it to the left of the formula bar's entry area. Click the Enter box now. Excel records the Date label in cell A1, and the indicator in the status bar changes back to *Ready*. Notice that the entry is left-aligned in its cell. Unless you tell Excel to do otherwise, it always left-aligns text entries and right-aligns numeric entries.

Recording entries with the Enter box

3. Click cell B1 to select it. The reference at the left end of the formula bar changes from A1 to B1, and the dark border that designates the active cell moves one cell to the right.

4. Type *Invoice Number*, but instead of clicking the Enter box to enter the label in the cell, press the Tab key. Excel records the entry in cell B1 and moves the active cell to C1.

5. Type *Salesperson*, and press Tab.

6. Now enter one more label. In cell D1, type *Amount of Sale*, and click the Enter box to record the entry. Here's how the worksheet looks with the newly entered row of labels:

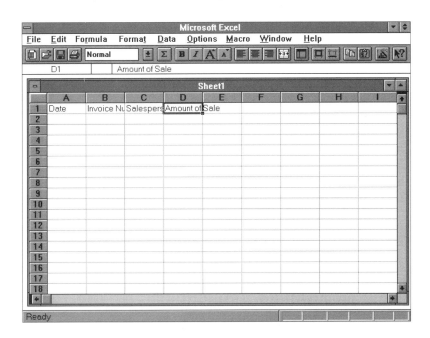

Long text entries ────────────► Notice that the labels in cells B1, C1, and D1 are too long to fit in their cells. Until you entered the Salesperson label in cell C1, the Invoice Number label spilled over into C1, just as Amount of Sale now spills over from D1 into E1. After you entered the Salesperson label, Excel truncated Invoice Number so that you could read the label in C1. Similarly, after you entered Amount of Sale, Excel truncated Salesperson. The Invoice Number and Salesperson labels are still intact in B1 and C1, however. (If you're skeptical, click either cell and look at the formula bar.) In a minute, you'll learn how to adjust column widths to accommodate long entries.

That's it for the column labels. Now let's turn our attention to the rest of the table. We'll skip the Date and Invoice Number columns for the moment and enter the names of a few salespeople in last-name/first-name order in column C.

1. Click cell C2 to select it, and type *Crux, Jamie*.

2. Instead of clicking the Enter box, press the Enter key. Excel records the entry in cell C2 and makes cell C3 the active cell. (If the active cell doesn't move, see the tip below.)

3. Type *Olderon, Sam* in cell C3, and press Enter to record the entry and move to cell C4.

4. Next, type the following names in the Salesperson column, pressing Enter after each one:

Two Enter keys

In Excel, the Enter key on the numeric keypad is functionally equivalent to the Enter key on the main keyboard.

Moving after pressing Enter

If pressing the Enter key does not move the active cell down one row after recording an entry, choose the Workspace command from the Options menu, select the Move Selection After Enter option, and click OK.

Using Alternate Navigation Keys

The Alternate Navigation Keys option in the Workspace dialog box provides additional keyboard shortcuts for worksheet navigation and formula entry. Many examples in this book will result in errors if this option is selected. For purposes of the examples provided here, leave this option deselected.

C4	Karnov, Peter
C5	Smite, Karleena
C6	Crux, Tad
C7	Furban, Wally
C8	Ladder, Larry
C9	Karnov, Peter
C10	Crux, Jamie
C11	Ladder, Larry
C12	Furban, Wally

Now let's enter the invoice numbers in column B. Usually, you will want Excel to treat invoice numbers—and social security numbers, part numbers, phone numbers, and other numbers that are used primarily for identification—as text rather than as numeric values on which you might want to perform calculations. If the "number" includes not only the digits 0 through 9 but also letters and other characters (such as hyphens), Excel usually recognizes it as text. However, if the number consists of only digits and you want Excel to treat it as text, you have to explicitly tell Excel to do so.

Entering numbers as text

For demonstration purposes, assume that your company has two regional offices, East and West. Both offices use invoice numbers with six characters. Invoices generated by the East office consist of four digits followed by AA, and those generated by the West office consist of six digits that end with 00 (two zeros). Follow the steps below to see how Excel treats these invoice numbers:

1. Click cell B2 to select it, type *4739AA*, and press Enter. This invoice number consists of both digits and letters, so Excel treats the entry as text and left-aligns it.

2. In cell B3, which is now active, type *943200*, and press Enter. This invoice number consists of only digits, so Excel treats the entry as a numeric value and right-aligns it in its cell.

How do you tell Excel to also treat the entry that consists of only digits as text? You type the entry as a text string by enclosing it in double quotation marks, and you precede the entry with an equal sign to tell Excel that the value of the cell is equal to the text string. Follow the steps on the next page.

1. Hold down the Shift key and press the Enter key to move back up to cell B3.

2. Type =*"943200"*, and press Enter. Excel overwrites the numeric value with the text entry and left-aligns the entry in its cell. (Although Excel has overwritten the numeric entry in B3 with a numeric entry in text form, the program can still recognize the entry as a number. If you refer to cell B3 in a formula, Excel treats the entry just like any other numeric entry.)

3. Enter these invoice numbers in the indicated cells, being sure to enter those that end in 00 as text strings:

B4	8488AA
B5	4398AA
B6	4945AA
B7	825600
B8	846500
B9	4409AA
B10	8867AA
B11	875600
B12	479300

   Your worksheet now looks like this:

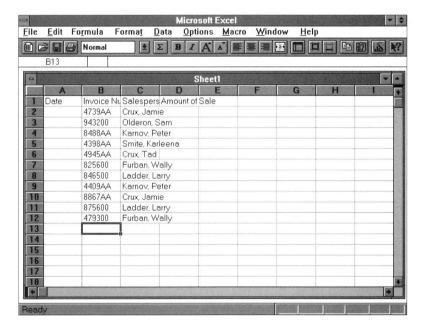

Entering Numeric Values

As you have seen, entering numeric values is just as easy as entering text. Follow along with the next few steps, as we enter the sales amounts in column D:

1. Click cell D2 to select the first cell in the Amount of Sale column, type *83456.23*, and press Enter. Excel records the entry and right-aligns it.

2. Enter the following amounts in the indicated cells, pressing the Enter key after each one:

D3	90875.56
D4	634568.30
D5	42356.07
D6	65643.90
D7	123456.45
D8	67345.23
D9	145768.34
D10	43256.23
D11	11256.90
D12	85345.00

   Don't worry if Excel does not display these values exactly as you entered them (see the tip below). On page 52, we format these amounts so that they display as dollars and cents.

Long numeric values

As you have seen, Excel allows a long text entry to overflow into an adjacent empty cell and truncates the entry only if the adjacent cell also contains an entry. However, the program treats a long numeric value differently. If Excel displays pound signs (###) instead of the value you entered, the value is too large to display in the cell, and you must make the column wider to view it. Non-dollar values are displayed in scientific notation, and values with many decimal places are rounded off. For example, if you enter 12345678912345 in a standard-width cell (which is 8.43 characters in width), Excel displays 123E+13 (123 times 10 to the 13th power). If you enter 123456.789 in a standard-width cell, Excel displays 123456.8. In both cases, Excel leaves the underlying value unchanged. You can widen the column to display some long numeric values the way you entered them. (Adjusting the width of columns is discussed on page 30.)

Entering Dates and Times

Entering in format

Even seasoned Excel users sometimes have difficulty entering dates and times in their worksheets. For dates and times
to be displayed correctly, you must enter them "in format,"
which means that you must enter them in a format that Excel
recognizes as either a date or time. The following formats are
recognized:

3/9/92	9:35 PM
9-Mar-92	9:35:43 PM
9-Mar	9:35
Mar-92	3-9-92 9:35

One additional format combines both date and time, and takes
this form:

3/9/91 9:35

Let's get a feel for how Excel handles different date formats:

1. Enter the following dates in the indicated cells, pressing Enter
after each one:

A2	Mar 9, 1992
A3	1/4/92
A4	Jan 10, 92
A5	January 16, 1992
A6	February 3, 1992
A7	2-8-92
A8	2/14/92
A9	3/2/92
A10	3-12-92
A11	23 Mar 1992
A12	March 30, 1992

Excel might display the date differently from the way you
entered it. Later, we'll come back and clean up the Date
column so that the dates all appear in the same format.

As you can see at the top of the next page, you have now completed all the columns of this simple worksheet.

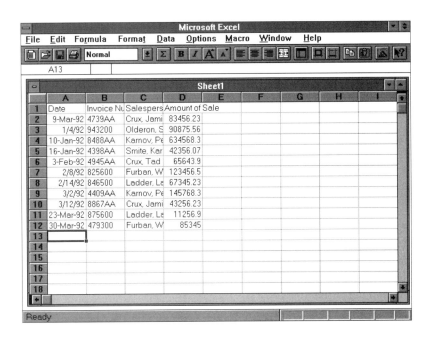

Selecting Ranges

Well, we've created a basic worksheet. But before we can show you some of the things you can do with it, we need to discuss how to select blocks of cells, called ranges. Any rectangular block or blocks containing more than one cell is a range. A range can include two cells, an entire row or column, or the entire worksheet. Knowing how to select and work with ranges saves you time, because you can apply formats to or reference the whole range, instead of having to deal with its component cells individually.

Ranges have references that are composed of the address of the cell in the top-left corner of the rectangular block and the address of the cell in the bottom-right corner, separated by a colon. For example, the reference A1:B2 identifies the range that consists of cells A1, A2, B1, and B2.

Referring to ranges of cells

The simplest way to learn how to select ranges is to actually do it, so follow along as we demonstrate selecting ranges of different shapes and sizes.

1. Point to cell A1, hold down the mouse button, and drag diagonally to cell D12 without releasing the button. Notice that the reference at the left end of the formula bar reads

12R x 4C, which indicates you are selecting a range of cells 12 rows high by 4 columns wide.

2. Release the mouse button. The range A1:D12 remains highlighted to indicate that it is selected. As you can see here, cell A1—the cell where you started the selection—is white, to indicate that it is the active cell in the range.

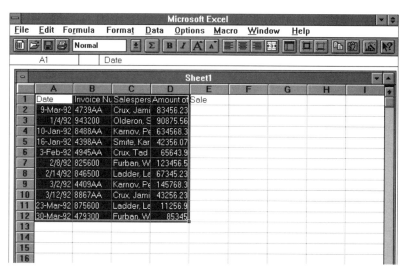

Selecting columns

3. Now move the mouse pointer to the heading of column B, and click. Excel simultaneously deselects A1:D12 and selects all of column B—the range B1:B16384.

4. Now point to the heading of column C, hold down the mouse button, and drag through the heading for column D. Before you release the button, notice that the reference in the formula bar reads *2C*, indicating that two entire columns—the range C1:D16384—are selected.

5. Move the pointer to the heading of row 6, and click to select the entire row—the range A6:IV6.

Next, try selecting ranges with the keyboard:

1. Select cell B6, hold down the Shift key, press the Right Arrow key twice and the Down Arrow key twice, and release the Shift key. The range B6:D8 is selected.

2. Select cell B6, hold down the Shift key, and then press the Spacebar. Row 6—the range A6:IV6—is selected.

Moving within a range

When a range is selected, pressing the Enter or Tab key moves the active cell within the range downward or to the right, respectively, without deselecting the range. Press the Enter or Tab key while holding down the Shift key to move the active cell upward or to the left within the range. Clicking any cell in the worksheet deselects the range.

3. Select cell B6, hold down the Ctrl key, and then press the Spacebar. Column B—the range B1:B16384—is selected.

The ranges you just selected were all single blocks of cells, but ranges can be more than one block. These ranges are referred to as discontinuous ranges. Try this:

1. Use any method to select the range A1:B2.

2. Hold down the Ctrl key, and use the mouse to select the range C4:D5. Your worksheet now looks like this:

Selecting discontinuous ranges

```
┌──────────────────────────────── Microsoft Excel ──────────────────────┬─┬─┐
│ File  Edit  Formula  Format  Data  Options  Macro  Window  Help                  │
├────────────────────────────────────────────────────────────────────────┤
│ [buttons] Normal  [Σ B I A A E E E E] [buttons]                               │
├────────────────────────────────────────────────────────────────────────┤
│   C4              │ Karnov, Peter                                            │
├──────────────────────── Sheet1 ──────────────────────────────────┬─┬─┤
│     A        B          C         D        E      F      G      H      I        │
│ 1 Date     Invoice Nu Salespers Amount of Sale                                 │
│ 2 9-Mar-92 4739AA    Crux, Jami  83456.23                                      │
│ 3  1/4/92   943200    Olderon, S  90875.56                                     │
│ 4 10-Jan-92 8488AA   Karnov, Pe  634568.3                                      │
│ 5 16-Jan-92 4398AA   Smite, Kar  42356.07                                      │
│ 6 3-Feb-92 4945AA    Crux, Tad   65643.9                                       │
│ 7  2/8/92   825600    Furban, W  123456.5                                      │
│ 8 2/14/92  846500    Ladder, Le  67345.23                                      │
│ 9  3/2/92   4409AA    Karnov, Pe 145768.3                                      │
│10 3/12/92  8867AA    Crux, Jami  43256.23                                      │
│11 23-Mar-92 875600   Ladder, Le  11256.9                                       │
│12 30-Mar-92 479300   Furban, W   85345                                         │
│13                                                                               │
│14                                                                               │
│15                                                                               │
│16                                                                               │
└────────────────────────────────────────────────────────────────────────┘
```

Notice that cell C4, the first cell of the second part of the range, is now the active cell.

Giving Excel Instructions

Now that you know how to select cells and ranges, let's quickly cover how you tell Excel what to do with your selection. You usually give Excel instructions by means of commands that are arranged in menus on the menu bar. Because this procedure is the same for all Windows applications, we assume that you are familiar with it and we provide only a quick review here. If you are a new Windows user, we suggest that you spend a little time becoming familiar with the mechanics of menus, commands, and dialog boxes before proceeding.

Goto selection shortcut

A quick way to select a large range without using the mouse is to choose the Goto command on the Formula menu and enter the range reference in the Reference text box. To select discontinuous ranges using this method, separate the range references with commas. For example, entering A1:B2, C4:D5 in the Goto dialog box selects those ranges. When you click OK, Excel scrolls to the range and selects it.

Choosing commands

To choose a command from a menu, you first click the name of the menu in the menu bar. When the menu drops down, you simply click the name of the command you want. From the keyboard, you can press Alt or the forward slash key (/) to activate the menu bar, press the underlined letter of the name of the menu, and then press the underlined letter of the command you want.

Some command names are occasionally displayed in "gray" letters, indicating that you can't choose the commands. For example, the Paste command on the Edit menu appears in gray until you have used the Cut or Copy command.

Dialog boxes

Some command names are followed by an ellipsis (...), indicating that you must supply more information before Excel can carry out the command. When you choose one of these commands, Excel displays a dialog box. You can then give the necessary information by typing in a text box or by selecting options from list boxes, drop-down list boxes, or groups of check boxes and option buttons. Clicking one of the command buttons—usually OK—closes the dialog box and carries out the command according to your specifications. Clicking Cancel closes the dialog box and also cancels the command. Other command buttons might be available to refine the original command or to open other dialog boxes with more options. Most dialog boxes also contain a Help button, which you use to get information about the dialog box.

Shortcut menus

More commands

Pressing the Shift key before you pull down menus can change some commands. For example, the Close command on the File menu becomes Close All when you hold down the Shift key, and the Fill Right and Fill Down commands on the Edit menu become Fill Left and Fill Up.

Shortcut menus are context-sensitive menus that group together frequently used editing and formatting commands. The menus appear when you click an object (such as a cell, a chart element, or a toolbar) using the right mouse button.

Toolbars

Excel 4 comes with 9 built-in toolbars, which you can customize to suit your needs. These include the Standard, Formatting, Utility, Chart, Drawing, Microsoft Excel 3.0, and Macro toolbars. You can also create your own toolbars. By default, the Standard toolbar is displayed, but you can hide or display any of the other toolbars, at the expense of screen space. Use the Toolbars command on the Options menu, or use the toolbar shortcut menu, to display or hide toolbars and customize them. After you become comfortable with using the toolbars, you might opt for creating your own, because many of the tools are repeated on different toolbars, and you might never use some tools. To find out how a toolbar tool works, press Shift-F1 or click the Help tool to activate context-sensitive help, and then click the tool in question.

You can also move and resize toolbars. Simply click anywhere on the toolbar (except on a button), and drag it away from the menu bar. The toolbar will turn into a floating palette, which you can resize like a window. Double-click the title bar on the palette to return the toolbar to its original position. The next time you move the toolbar, it will return to its previous resized shape.

Keyboard Shortcuts

If you and your mouse don't get along and you prefer to use the keyboard, you can access many Excel commands by means of keyboard shortcuts. The list of shortcuts is extensive, and it would take a lot of space to reproduce it here. You can display the list by choosing the Contents command from the Help menu and then clicking the Keyboard Guide.

Saving Worksheets

With that brief overview out of the way, let's turn our attention back to the worksheet we have created and find out how to save it for future use. Follow these steps:

1. Click the Save File tool on the toolbar to display the Save As dialog box so that you can name the worksheet.

2. In the File Name text box, Excel suggests SHEET1.XLS as the name of the file. Overwrite this suggestion by typing *sales*. There's no need to supply an extension, because Excel automatically adds the extension XLS to indicate that the file is an Excel spreadsheet.

3. Leave the other settings in the dialog box as they are for now, and click OK to carry out the command.

When you return to the Excel window, notice that the name SALES.XLS has replaced Sheet1 in the worksheet's title bar.

Saving existing worksheets

From now on, when you click the Save File tool to save changes to this worksheet, Excel will not display the Save As dialog box because it already knows the name of the worksheet. Excel simply saves the worksheet by overwriting the previous version with the new version.

Preserving previous versions

If you want to save the changes you have made to a worksheet but preserve the previous version, you can assign the new version a different name by choosing the Save As command from the File menu, entering the new name in the File Name text box, and clicking OK.

Creating New Worksheets

Having saved our worksheet, let's create a new one so that we can see how to work with more than one document at the same time. Follow these steps:

1. Click the New File tool on the toolbar.

2. Click OK to create a new worksheet. (We talk about creating new charts on page 110, workbooks on page 131, and macro sheets on page 141.) Excel opens a new blank worksheet with the name Sheet2, overlapping SALES.XLS. Your screen looks like this:

File-naming conventions

DOS file-naming conventions apply to Excel worksheet names. The names you assign your worksheets must be eight characters or less and can include letters, numbers, and the following characters:

_ ^ $! # % & - { } ( )

They cannot contain spaces, commas, or periods.

Saving in another directory

By default, the worksheet will be saved in the directory in which you installed Excel. To save the worksheet in a different directory, simply select the directory you want from the Directories list in the Save As dialog box before clicking OK.

Opening multiple files

You can use the File Open dialog box to open several files at once. Simply click the Open File tool on the toolbar, hold down the Ctrl key, and click the names of the files you want to open. When you click OK, Excel opens each selected worksheet in its own window. You can have many files open at one time, but we've found that four is the practical limit if you want to be able to see them all and do useful work.

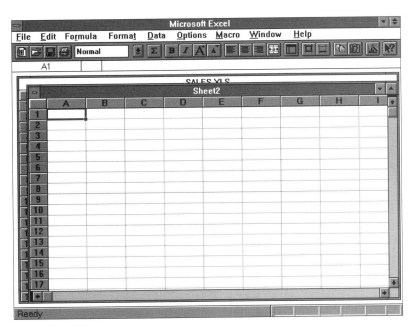

That's all there is to it. You now have two worksheets open on your screen with which to experiment.

Manipulating Windows

Let's take a moment to review some window basics. Being able to work with more than one worksheet open at a time is useful, especially if you frequently need to use the same set of numbers in different worksheets. For example, you might use the same raw data to develop a budget, work out a trial balance, or create an income statement. Follow the steps on the next page to see how easy it is to move among worksheets.

Save options

Clicking the Options button in the Save As dialog box displays several more options. Selecting the Create Backup File option causes Excel to create a copy of the previously saved version of the worksheet before overwriting it with the new version. Excel gives the backup copy the extension BAK. You can return to the previous version of a worksheet by opening the backup copy.

You can assign a password of up to 15 characters in the Protection Password text box. Excel then requires that the password be entered correctly before it will open the worksheet. The Write Reservation Password option works the same way, except that Excel opens a read-only version of the worksheet without requiring the password. The read-only version can be altered but can be saved only with a different name. Selecting the Read-Only Recommended option warns users that the worksheet should be opened as read-only. Excel does not, however, prevent users from opening the worksheet in the usual way.

1. Click any visible part of SALES.XLS to make it the active worksheet. If you can't see SALES.XLS, choose it from the list of open documents at the bottom of the Window menu. Notice that the color of its title bar changes to indicate that it is the active worksheet.

Arranging windows

2. Choose Arrange from the Window menu, and click OK in the Arrange Windows dialog box. Excel arranges the two worksheets so that they each occupy half the screen, like this:

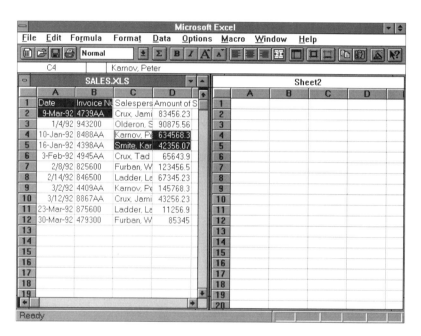

Minimizing to icons

Just as you can minimize group windows to icons in Program Manager, you can do the same with document windows in Excel. In this way, you can keep many documents open at the same time without cluttering up the screen, or obscuring other documents.

Scroll bars

The right scroll bar moves the worksheet up and down, and the bottom scroll bar moves the worksheet left and right. To move quickly to other parts of the worksheet, hold down the Shift key and drag the scroll boxes. The column and row references in the formula bar will change rapidly. Release the mouse button when the reference reaches the column or row you want to view. Drag the scroll boxes to the ends of the scroll bars to display cell IV16384.

Using the scroll bars to bring cells into view does not change the active cell. As a result, you can pause in the middle of making an entry to view a cell in a different area of the worksheet and then return to the active cell with your incomplete entry still in the formula bar, just as you left it. No matter where you scroll to in a worksheet, the minute you begin typing, you return instantly to the active cell.

3. Click anywhere in Sheet2 to make it the active worksheet. Notice that scroll bars appear only in the active window. Any entries you make and any commands you choose will now affect only this worksheet.

4. Click the Maximize button (the upward-pointing arrow at the right end of Sheet2's title bar). Sheet2 expands to fill the screen, completely obscuring SALES.XLS.

Maximizing windows

5. Pull down the Window menu again. Notice that the names of the two open worksheets appear at the bottom of the menu. A check mark indicates the active one.

6. Choose SALES.XLS from the Window menu. The two worksheets switch places, and SALES.XLS now completely obscures Sheet 2. (Where you maximize one window, all of the windows in the "stack" of windows become maximized.)

Editing Basics

In this section, we briefly cover some simple ways of revising and manipulating worksheets so that in subsequent chapters we can give general editing instructions without having to go into great detail.

Changing Entries

First, let's see how to change individual entries. Glancing at the Amount of Sale column in SALES.XLS, notice that the

---

Keyboard shortcuts

You can use the keyboard to move around the worksheet. You'll use the Tab and Enter keys most often, but as you gain more experience with Excel you might find other keys useful. (Note that navigating with the keyboard always relocates the active cell.) Here's a list of navigation keys and what they do:

Key	Action	Key	Action
Enter	Moves active cell down one cell.	Shift-Enter	Moves active cell up one cell.
Tab	Moves active cell right one cell.	Shift-Tab	Moves active cell left one cell.
Home	Moves active cell to column A in current row.	Ctrl-Home	Moves active cell to cell A1.
End	Activates "End mode." Press an arrow key after End to move to beginning or end of current row, column, or region.	Ctrl-End	Moves active cell to the cell in the bottom-right corner of the current region, defined as the rectangular area containing cells.
Page Up	Moves screen up one screenful and activates a cell in screen's top row.		
Page Down	Moves screen down one screenful and activates a cell in screen's top row.		

amount in cell D4 is suspiciously large compared with all the other amounts. Suppose that you check this number and find to your disappointment that the amount should be 63456.83, not 634568.3. Here's how you make the correction without having to retype the entire number:

1. Select cell D4.

2. Move the pointer to the formula bar between the 6 and the 8, and click. Excel creates a blinking insertion point between the two numbers and the indicator in the status bar changes to EDIT.

3. Type a period (.).

4. Click between the second period and the 3, and then press Backspace to delete the second period.

5. Press Enter to record the corrected entry in the cell.

Copying Entries

You can copy an entry or group of entries anywhere within the same worksheet or to a different worksheet. Copy operations involve the use of two commands: Copy and Paste (or Insert Paste). Follow these steps:

1. Select A1:D12, and click the Copy tool on the toolbar. A dotted rectangle, called a marquee, surrounds the selection, like this:

The Clipboard	Temporary storage	Clipboard contents
The Windows Clipboard is a temporary storage space used to hold cut or copied data from all Windows applications. You can also use it to transfer data from the documents of one application to those of another.	Because the Windows Clipboard is a temporary storage space, exiting Windows or turning off your computer erases any information that is stored there, unless you save the Clipboard file. Save the file by switching to Program Manager, double-clicking the Clipboard icon (or the Clipboard Viewer icon) to display the Clipboard window, and choosing Save from the File menu.	If you cut or copy cells and then double-click the Clipboard icon (or the Clipboard Viewer) in Program Manager, instead of displaying a copy of the cells and their contents, the Clipboard indicates the cut or copied range size. For example, *Copy 3R x 3C* indicates a range three rows high by three columns wide. This display has no effect on the result of pasting the cut or copied cells, however.

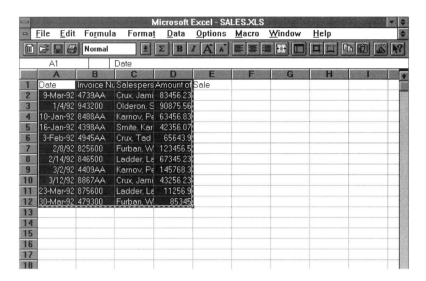

2. Select cell E1, and choose Paste from the Edit menu.

   Notice that you do not have to select a range of cells in which to paste the copied range. Excel assumes that the selected cell is the location of the top-left corner of the paste area. Also notice that the marquee still surrounds the original selection, indicating that you can paste another copy of the entries if necessary, even though the range E1:H12 is now selected.

   Another way to cut and paste cells is to use Excel 4's short-cut menus.

1. Select cell F1, and click it again using the right mouse button. This shortcut menu pops up:

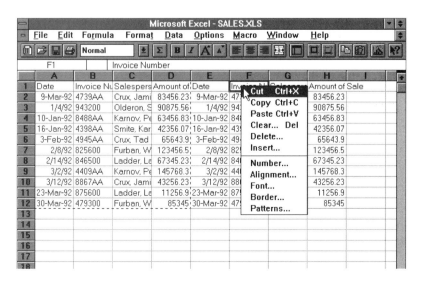

2. Choose Paste from the shortcut menu. Again, Excel uses the selected cell as the top-left corner of the paste area and, without warning, pastes the entries over the existing contents of cells F1:I12.

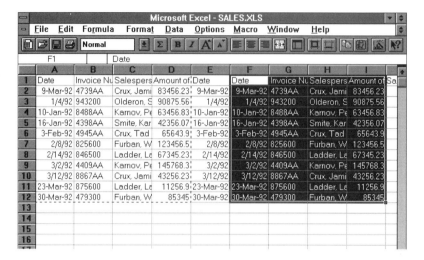

Cause for panic? Not at all. Excel's Undo command is designed for just such an occasion.

Undoing commands

3. Choose Undo Paste from the Edit menu. Excel restores your worksheet to its prepaste status.

Excel 4 provides another way to cut, copy, and paste cells within a worksheet using a simple mouse operation.

Copying with Cell Drag And Drop

1. First, choose Workspace from the Options menu, and in the Workspace Options dialog box, check that the Cell Drag And Drop option is turned on. Click OK to close the dialog box. Reselect A1:D12, and then move the pointer to the range border.

2. When the pointer changes to a left-pointing arrow, press the Ctrl key. A small plus sign appears next to the pointer, indicating that Excel is ready to copy and paste.

3. While holding down the Ctrl key, click the mouse button, and drag the outline of the selection over the range E1:H12.

4. Release the mouse button and the Ctrl key. Excel pastes a copy of the selected cells into the destination range.

The result of this operation is identical to using the Copy and Paste commands. However, because Excel doesn't place a copy of the selected range on the Clipboard, you can use this technique to copy and paste only within a single worksheet. Because Cell Drag And Drop editing requires that you hold down both the Ctrl key and the mouse button, it's probably best reserved for copying and pasting small ranges a short distance from the original.

1. Let's try another technique for copying and pasting cells. Copy the range A1:D12 again, and select cell E1.

2. Choose Insert Paste from the Edit menu. Excel displays this dialog box:

Choosing the Insert Paste command tells Excel to paste in the copied range, inserting enough cells to accommodate the entries without overwriting any existing cell contents. Excel wants to know in which direction it should move the existing cells, guessing that you will want to move them to the right, because the copied range has more rows than columns.

3. Click OK. Excel proceeds with the paste operation, inserting a second copy of A1:D12 between the original and the first copy, as shown here:

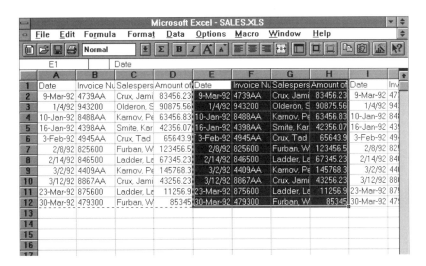

Notice that the first copy of the range has shifted to cells I1:L12. The marquee still surrounds the original range, so let's make yet another copy, this time in Sheet2.

1. Choose Sheet2 from the bottom of the Window menu, and check that cell A1 is active.

2. Choose Paste from either the Edit menu or the cell shortcut menu. Excel faithfully pastes in a copy of the range from SALES.XLS.

Moving Entries

The procedure for moving cell entries is similar to that for copying entries. In this case, you use two commands: Cut and Paste (or Insert Paste). Try this:

1. Choose the Arrange command from the Window menu, and click OK in the Arrange Windows dialog box to display both open worksheets.

2. Activate SALES.XLS, and use the bottom scroll bar to move columns E through H into view.

3. Select E1:H12 in SALES.XLS, and choose Cut from either the Edit menu or the cell shortcut menu. Excel surrounds the selection with a marquee.

4. Select A13 in Sheet2. Then either choose Paste from the Edit menu, choose Paste from the cell shortcut menu, or press Enter (all methods work identically). Excel moves the entries

Hiding windows

Use the Hide command on the Window menu to hide the active window. For example, you might want to hide one or more of the open windows before choosing Arrange All. If the window is a macro sheet, all macros on the sheet are active even though it is not visible. Choose Unhide to make the window reappear.

Copying vs. moving

Remember, if you want to copy a range of cells using Cell Drag And Drop editing, hold down the Ctrl key while dragging the mouse. If you want to move the cells, simply drag, without holding down an additional key.

from E1:H12 of SALES.XLS into A13:D24 of Sheet2. Your worksheets now look like this:

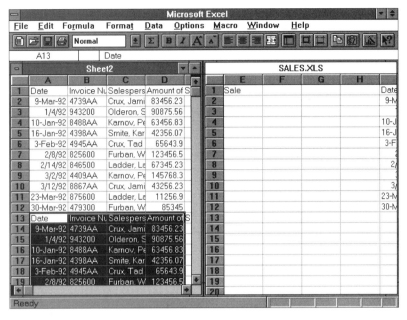

5. To get a better view of the results in SALES.XLS, activate the window, and click its Maximize button.

6. Pull down the Edit menu, and notice that the Paste command is gray and unavailable. Unlike copied entries, you can paste cut entries only once.

   You can also use Cell Drag And Drop editing to move a range within a single worksheet. Try this:

1. Select A1:D12, and move the pointer to the border of the range, where it changes to a left-pointing arrow.

Moving with Cell Drag And Drop

2. Drag the range outline to a new location in the worksheet, and release the mouse button. If the destination range has no cell entries, the selected range simply moves to its new location. If any of the cells in the destination range contain entries, Excel displays the message *Overwrite non blank cells in destination?* Click OK to overwrite the cells, or click Cancel to undo the Cell Drag And Drop operation.

3. Choose Undo Drag And Drop from the Edit menu to undo this editing action.

Clearing Cells

Let's tidy up SALES.XLS by getting rid of the extraneous copy of your data. You need to erase the entries in cells I1:L12—in Excel jargon, you need to *clear the cells*. Clearing cells is different from cutting entries: Cutting entries assumes that you will paste the entries somewhere else, whereas clearing cells simply erases the entries. Here's how you clear cells:

1. Select I1:L12, and choose Clear from either the Edit menu or the cell shortcut menu. Excel displays this dialog box:

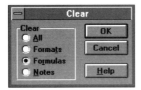

The default option in the Clear dialog box is Formulas. For this type of operation, Excel considers all cell entries to be formulas, even text and numeric entries that don't involve any computations. You can use the other options to clear any formats and notes you have assigned to cells, but in this case, the default option is just what you need.

2. Click OK. Excel clears the cells, and your worksheet now looks as it did before you started copying and moving.

Inserting and Deleting Cells

It is a rare person who can create a worksheet from scratch without ever having to tinker with its design—moving this block of data, changing that label, or adding or deleting a column here and there. In this section, we'll show you how to insert and delete cells. Follow these steps:

Inserting columns

1. Click the column D heading to select the entire column.

2. Choose Insert from either the Edit menu or the cell shortcut menu. Excel inserts an entire blank column in front of the Amount of Sale column which, as you can see on the following page, is now column E:

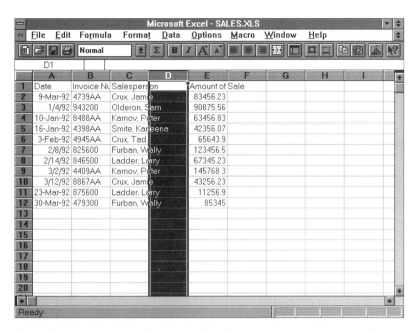

Inserting rows

Inserting a row works exactly the same way as inserting a column. You simply click the row heading and choose Insert from either the Edit or the cell shortcut menu.

What if you need to insert only a few cells and inserting an entire column will mess up some of your entries? You can insert cells anywhere you need them, as you'll see if you follow these steps:

1. Select E1:E10—all but two of the cells containing entries in column E—and choose Insert from either the Edit menu or the cell shortcut menu. Excel displays this dialog box:

Because you have selected a range rather than the entire column, Excel needs to know which cells to move to make room for the inserted cells.

2. Click OK to accept the default option of shifting cells to the right. Excel inserts a new blank cell to the left of each selected cell, as shown on the next page.

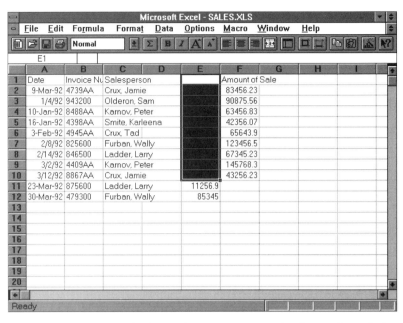

You could undo this insertion to restore the integrity of the Amount of Sale column, but instead let's delete E1:E10:

1. With E1:E10 selected, choose Delete from either the Edit menu or the cell shortcut menu. Excel displays a Delete dialog box similar to the Insert dialog box to find out how to close up the space that will be left by the deleted cells.

2. Click OK to accept the default option of shifting cells to the left. Excel deletes the cells, and the sale amounts are now back in one column.

You can also insert and delete using Drag And Drop editing, like this:

Inserting with Cell Drag And Drop

1. Select C1:C12, and move the pointer to the small black box in the bottom-right corner of the range border. The pointer changes to a dark cross hair.

2. Hold down the Shift key, and drag the range outline one column to the right. Excel inserts a range of blank cells between the selected cells in column C and the information that was in column E.

Deleting with Cell Drag And Drop

3. Hold down the Shift key, and drag the dark cross-hair pointer one column to the left. Excel deletes the inserted blank cells and restores column E to its original state.

You can leave the empty column D where it is for now—
you'll use it when we work with SALES.XLS again in the next
chapter.

Formatting Basics

Excel offers a wide variety of formatting options that allow
you to emphasize parts of your worksheets and display data
in different ways. Here we'll look at the formatting options
that are available on the Standard toolbar. We'll also show
you a quick way to adjust column widths. Later, when you
have more Excel experience, you might want to explore the
formatting options available on the Format menu.

Changing Worksheet Formatting

Just as you can use labels to make tables of data easier to read,
you can use formatting to distinguish different categories of
information. You could spend a lot of time manually formatting a table to get it to look perfect. Fortunately, Excel 4
provides some tools that make formatting a snap.

1. Select the range A1:E12.

2. Click the AutoFormat tool on the toolbar. Excel instantly
   formats the range as shown here:

Automatic formatting

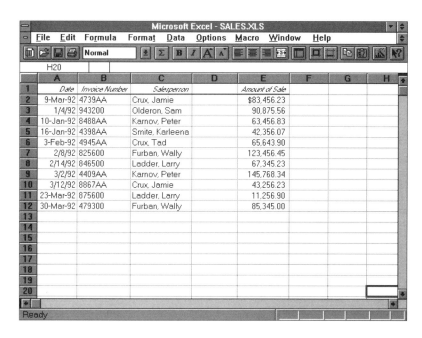

Excel has right-aligned and italicized the labels at the top of the columns, made the columns wide enough to display the entire cell entries, and added a border below the labels to set them off. (If you click one of the cells containing labels, you will see that the Italic and Right Align tools on the toolbar appear "pressed," indicating that these formats are in effect for the selected cell.) Excel has also formatted the values in column E so that each has two decimal places and has formatted the first value in the column as currency. Making all these changes manually would have meant using tools on the toolbar or options in the Font, Border, Alignment, and Column Width dialog boxes.

To further enhance the table, try the following:

1. Click row 1's heading to select the row containing the labels.

Adding bold

2. Click the Bold tool on the toolbar. The labels are now bold.

Because you have formatted the entire row, any entries you make in row 1 will be bold. (Although you can copy or cut and paste formatting along with entries, it is the cell that is actually formatted, not the entry.)

Changing Column Widths

Because making the labels bold made some of the labels spill over into adjacent columns, you'll want to adjust the widths of columns B and E so that the labels fit neatly in their cells. Here's what you do:

1. Move the mouse pointer to the dividing line between the heading of column B and that of column C. The pointer shape changes to a vertical bar with two opposing arrows:

AutoFormat options

The AutoFormat dialog box has fourteen colorful table types to choose from. To quickly cycle through these formats, select the range to be formatted, and hold down the Shift key while clicking the AutoFormat tool. If you make formatting changes to a table created with the AutoFormat tool and then decide you don't like the changes, you can quickly reformat the table by clicking the AutoFormat tool again.

	A	B	C	D	E	F	G	H
1	*Date*	*voice Number*	*Salesperson*		*Amount of Sale*			
2	9-Mar-92	4739AA	Crux, Jamie		$83,456.23			
3	1/4/92	943200	Olderon, Sam		90,875.56			
4	10-Jan-92	8488AA	Karnov, Peter		63,456.83			
5	16-Jan-92	4398AA	Smite, Karleena		42,356.07			
6	3-Feb-92	4945AA	Crux, Tad		65,643.90			
7	2/8/92	825600	Furban, Wally		123,456.45			
8	2/14/92	846500	Ladder, Larry		67,345.23			
9	3/2/92	4409AA	Karnov, Peter		145,768.34			
10	3/12/92	8867AA	Crux, Jamie		43,256.23			
11	23-Mar-92	875600	Ladder, Larry		11,256.90			

Microsoft Excel - SALES.XLS

File   Edit   Formula   Format   Data   Options   Macro   Window   Help

A1   Date

2. Hold down the mouse button, and drag to the right until column B is wide enough to display the Invoice Number label. Notice as you drag the border that the width of the column is displayed at the left end of the formula bar. Release the mouse button when you think that the text will fit into the cell.

Now widen column E using a different method:

1. Click the column E heading to select the column, and choose Column Width from either the Format menu or the shortcut menu. Excel displays this dialog box:

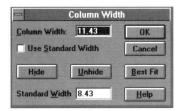

Using the Column Width command

The column's current width is displayed in the Column Width text box.

2. Click the Best Fit button. Excel increases the width of the column so that the Amount of Sale label is displayed in its entirety.

Your finished worksheet looks like the one shown on the following page.

A quick "Best Fit"

Use the Best Fit button in the Column Width dialog box to adjust a column's width so that it becomes just wide enough to hold the longest cell entry in the selected cells. To adjust the column width according to all cells in the column, select the entire column before you click the Best Fit button, or double-click the right border of the column heading.

Standard Width

By default, the standard width of a worksheet cell is 8.43, or about 8½ characters wide. To change the standard width of an entire worksheet, choose the Column Width command from the Format menu, enter a new width in the Standard Width text box, and then click OK.

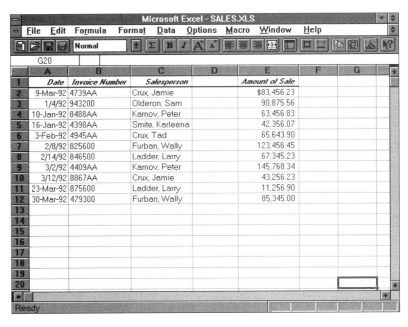

Adjusting row height →

You can adjust the height of rows the same way you adjust the width of columns. Simply drag the bottom border of the row heading up or down, or choose Row Height from the Format menu to make the row shorter or taller.

Getting Help

This tour of Excel has covered a lot of ground in a few pages, and you might be wondering how you will manage to retain it all. Don't worry. If you forget how to carry out a particular task, help is never far away. For example, let's see how you would remind yourself of how to save a worksheet:

Context-sensitive help →

1. Click the Help button, or press Shift-F1. A question mark appears next to the arrow pointer.

2. Choose Save from the File menu. Instead of actually saving the document, Excel displays this Help screen:

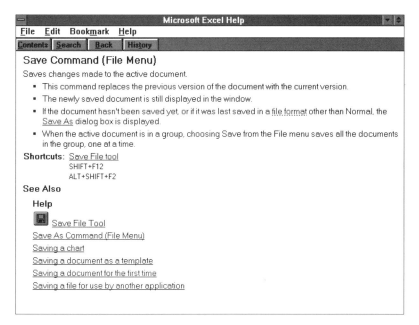

3. Click the Contents button to display a list of topics, which provide information on almost every aspect of Excel.

4. Choose Exit from Help's File menu to return to your worksheet window.

Quitting Excel

Well, that's it for the basic tour. All that's left is to show you how to end an Excel session. Follow these steps:

1. Choose Exit from the File menu.

2. When Excel asks whether you want to save the changes you have made to the open worksheets, click Yes for SALES.XLS, and click No for Sheet2.

2
Analyzing Income

Print Preview
Page 61

Zooming in and out
Page 62

Adjusting margins and column widths
Page 64

Repeating characters
Page 45

Applying styles
Page 52

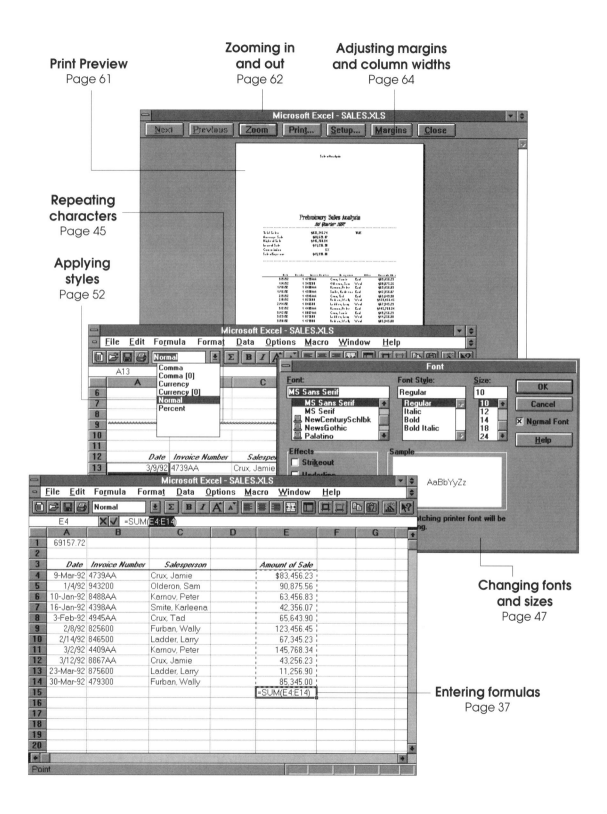

Changing fonts and sizes
Page 47

Entering formulas
Page 37

C hapter 1 covered some Excel basics, and you now know enough to create simple tables. But you are missing the essential piece of information that turns a table into a worksheet: how to enter formulas. The whole purpose of building worksheets is to have Excel perform calculations for you. In this chapter, we show you how to retrieve the SALES.XLS worksheet and enter formulas to analyze sales. (If you don't work in sales, you can adapt the worksheet to analyze other sources of income, such as service fees.) Along the way, you learn some powerful techniques for manipulating your data, and we cover the principles of worksheet design. Finally, we print the SALES.XLS worksheet. So fire up Excel, and we'll get started.

Opening Existing Worksheets

When you first start Excel, the worksheet window contains a blank document entitled Sheet1. You can open a worksheet you have already created using a couple of methods. If the worksheet is one of the last four you have worked with, you can simply choose the file from the bottom of the File menu. Otherwise, you can use the Open command, also on the File menu, or the Open File tool on the Standard toolbar to retrieve the worksheet. We'll use the first method:

Closing worksheets

1. If a blank Sheet1 is displayed on your screen, conserve your computer's memory by closing it. Simply choose Close from the File menu.

2. Now pull down the File menu, and choose SALES.XLS from the bottom of the menu. Excel displays the table you created in Chapter 1.

3. Click the worksheet's Maximize button to make the worksheet as large as possible.

Simple Calculations

Excel has many powerful functions that are a sort of shorthand for the various formulas used in mathematical, statistical, financial, trigonometric, logical, logarithmic, and other types of calculations. However, the majority of worksheets created with Excel involve simple arithmetic. In this section, we show you how to use the four arithmetic operators (+, −, *, and /) to add, subtract, multiply, and divide, and then we introduce two Excel features with which you can quickly add sets of numeric values.

Doing Arithmetic

You must begin all formulas you enter in Excel with an equal sign (=). In the simplest formulas, the equal sign is followed by a set of values separated by +, −, *, or /, such as

=5+3+2

If you type this formula in any blank cell in your worksheet and then press Enter, Excel displays the result 10.

Let's experiment with a few formulas. We'll start by inserting a couple of blank rows:

1. Click the row 1 heading, and drag down to the row 2 heading to select the two rows.

Inserting rows

2. Click anywhere in the selected rows using the right mouse button, and choose Insert from the shortcut menu. Because you selected two rows, Excel inserts two blank rows above the table, moving the table down so that it begins in row 3.

Now we're ready to construct a formula in cell A1, using some of the values in the Amount of Sale column. We could retype these values in the formula bar to create the formula, but instead we'll tell Excel to use a value simply by clicking the cell that contains it. Follow these steps:

1. Click cell A1, and type an equal sign followed by an opening parenthesis.

Entering formulas

2. Click cell E4. Excel inserts the cell reference E4 in the formula bar.

3. Type a plus sign, and click cell E5. Excel adds the cell reference E5 to the formula.

4. Continue to build the formula by typing plus signs and clicking cells E6, E7, and E8.

5. Type a closing parenthesis followed by a / (the division operator), and then type 5. The formula bar looks like this:

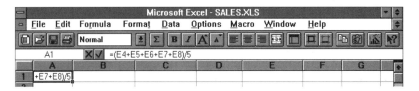

This formula tells Excel to first add the amounts in cells E4, E5, E6, E7, and E8 and then divide the result by 5, to obtain the average of the five amounts.

6. Click the Enter box. Excel displays the result of the formula, 69157.72, in cell A1. Notice that the formula also remains in the formula bar.

You can use the same technique to create any simple formula. Just type an equal sign, and then type a value or click the cell that contains the value, type the appropriate arithmetic operator, enter the next value, and so on. Unless you tell Excel to do otherwise, the program performs multiplication and division before addition and subtraction. If you need parts of the formula to be carried out in a specific order, use parentheses as we did in this calculation to override the default order.

Totaling Columns of Values

Although this method of creating a formula is simple enough, it would be tedious to have to type and click to create long formulas. Fortunately, Excel automates the process of totaling a series of numeric values with a very useful tool: the AutoSum tool on the Standard toolbar.

Using the AutoSum Tool   The AutoSum tool will probably become your most often-used Excel tool. Using this tool is so easy that we'll dispense with explanations and simply show you how:

1. Click cell E15 to select it, and then click the AutoSum tool. Excel looks above and to the left of the active cell for the largest range of numeric values to total. Because there are no values to the left of cell E15, Excel assumes that you want to total the values above it. Excel then enters a SUM function in

cell E15. (We discuss the SUM function next.) Your worksheet now looks like this:

	Microsoft Excel - SALES.XLS							
File	Edit	Formula	Format	Data	Options	Macro	Window	Help

| | Normal | | Σ | B | I | A˄ | A˅ | |

| E4 | X ✓ | =SUM(E4:E14) |

	A	B	C	D	E	F	G
1	69157.72						
2							
3	Date	Invoice Number	Salesperson		Amount of Sale		
4	9-Mar-92	4739AA	Crux, Jamie		$83,456.23		
5	1/4/92	943200	Olderon, Sam		90,875.56		
6	10-Jan-92	8488AA	Karnov, Peter		63,456.83		
7	16-Jan-92	4398AA	Smite, Karleena		42,356.07		
8	3-Feb-92	4945AA	Crux, Tad		65,643.90		
9	2/8/92	825600	Furban, Wally		123,456.45		
10	2/14/92	846500	Ladder, Larry		67,345.23		
11	3/2/92	4409AA	Karnov, Peter		145,768.34		
12	3/12/92	8867AA	Crux, Jamie		43,256.23		
13	23-Mar-92	875600	Ladder, Larry		11,256.90		
14	30-Mar-92	479300	Furban, Wally		85,345.00		
15					=SUM(E4:E14)		
16							

2. Click the Enter box to enter the formula in cell E15. Excel displays the result $822,216.74—the sum of the values in E4:E14—formatting the answer as currency, because the first value in the range is formatted as currency.

Well, that was easy. The AutoSum tool will serve you well whenever you want a total to appear at the bottom of a column or to the right of a row of numeric values. But what if you want the total to appear elsewhere on the worksheet? Knowing how to create SUM functions from scratch gives you more flexibility.

Using the SUM Function   Let's go back and dissect the SUM function that Excel inserted in cell E15 when you clicked the AutoSum tool so that you can see the function's components. Clicking cell E15 puts this entry in the formula bar:

=SUM(E4:E14)

Like all formulas, the SUM function begins with an equal sign. Next comes the function name in capital letters, followed by a set of parentheses enclosing the reference of the range containing the amounts you want to total. This reference is the SUM function's argument. An argument answers questions such as "What?" or "How?" and gives Excel the additional information it needs to perform the function. In the case of SUM, Excel needs only one piece of information—the

Function syntax

references of the cells you want it to total. As you'll see later in this chapter, Excel might need several pieces of information to carry out other functions, and you enter an argument for each piece.

Creating a SUM formula from scratch is not particularly difficult. To see how, follow these steps:

1. Select cell A1, and type this:

=SUM(

When you select a cell and begin typing, any value already in the cell is overwritten.

2. Select E4:E14. Excel inserts the range reference after the opening parenthesis.

3. Type a closing parenthesis, and click the Enter box. Excel displays a series of pound signs in the cell because the cell is not wide enough to display the entire result of the formula. When you make the column wider, you'll see that the result is the same as the one in cell E15—$822,216.74.

Using References to Formula Cells in Other Formulas

After you create a formula in one cell, you can use its result in other formulas simply by referencing its cell. To see how this works, follow these steps:

1. Select cell B1, and type an equal sign.

Displaying formulas

By default, Excel displays the results of formulas in cells, not the underlying formulas. To see the actual underlying formulas in the worksheet, choose Display from the Options menu, select the Formulas option, and click OK. Excel widens the cells so that you can view the formulas. Simply select the Formulas option again to redisplay the results.

Function names

When you type a function name such as SUM in the formula bar, you don't have to type it in capital letters. Excel capitalizes the function name for you when you finish entering the function. If Excel doesn't respond in this way, you have probably entered the function name or its syntax incorrectly.

Closing parenthesis

In a simple formula like the one above, you can omit the closing parenthesis because Excel adds it for you when you click the Enter box. When you do enter a closing parenthesis, however, Excel briefly makes the pair of parentheses bold in the formula bar. This feature can help you locate related sets of parentheses in long formulas, or in formulas nested within one another.

2. Click cell A1, which contains the SUM function you just entered, type a / (the division operator), and then type *11*.

3. Click the Enter box. Excel displays the result—the average of the invoice amounts—in cell B1.

Naming Cells and Ranges

Many of the calculations that you might want to perform on this worksheet—for example, calculating each invoice amount as a percentage of total sales—will use the total you have just entered in cell A1. You could include a copy of the SUM function now in cell A1 in these other calculations, or you could reference cell A1. The latter method seems quick and simple, but what if you subsequently move the formula in cell A1 to another location. Excel gives you a way to reference this formula, no matter where you move it. You can assign cell A1 a name and then use the name in any calculations that involve the total.

You assign a name to a cell with the Define Name command on the Formula menu. Follow these steps:

1. Select cell A1, and choose Define Name from the Formula menu. Excel displays the Define Name dialog box:

                                                              Defining names

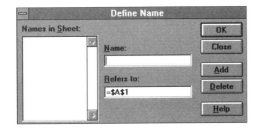

The reference for cell A1 is displayed in the Refers To text box with dollar signs in front of its column and row components. These dollar signs tell Excel that the cell reference is absolute, meaning that you will be able to use the name to refer to cell A1 from anywhere on the worksheet. (We discuss relative and absolute cell references later in this chapter, on page 60.)

2. Type the name *Total* in the Name box, and click OK. If you look at the cell reference area of the formula bar, you'll see

that Excel now refers to the cell by the name you just entered, instead of as A1. You can use either designation in formulas.

To see how Excel uses names, try this:

Using names

1. Click cell E15, which currently contains the SUM function inserted when you clicked the AutoSum tool earlier in the chapter.

2. Type =*Total*, and press Enter to record the entry in the cell. The worksheet does not appear to have changed, but now instead of two SUM functions, the worksheet contains only one: You have told Excel to assign the value of the cell named Total, which contains the SUM function, to cell E15.

You can also assign names to cell ranges. Let's assign the name Amount_of_Sale to the cells containing amounts in column E.

1. Select E3:E14, and choose Define Name from the Formula menu. Again, Excel displays the Define Name dialog box.

Cell-naming conventions

Certain rules apply when you name cells or ranges. Although you can use a number within the name, you must start the name with a letter. Also, spaces are not allowed within the name. Use underscore characters (_) to represent any spaces. For example, you cannot use 1992 as a name, but you can use Totals_1992.

Unique names

If you create a table with column labels across the top and row labels in the leftmost column, you can tell Excel to give each cell a unique name by combining the column and row labels. Select the entire table, choose Create Names from the Formula menu, select the Top Row and Left Column options, and click OK.

Linking with names

You can use names to refer to cells and ranges in other worksheets, even ones that are not currently open. See page 122 for more information about linking worksheets in this way.

Excel scans the range and guesses that you want to assign the label above the range as its name—Amount_of_Sale, in this case. (Notice that Excel replaces the spaces in the label with underscore characters.)

2. Click OK to assign the name.

Now let's replace the range reference in the SUM function in cell A1 with the new range name:

1. Click A1 to select it and display its contents in the formula bar.

2. Drag through the E4:E14 reference to highlight it.

3. Choose Paste Name from the Formula menu. Excel displays **Pasting names** the Paste Name dialog box:

4. Select Amount_of_Sale from the Paste Name list, and click OK. The name replaces the reference in the SUM function.

5. Click the Enter box. The total in cell A1 remains the same because the name Amount_of_Sale and the reference E4:E14 both refer to the same range.

Efficient Data Display

Before we discuss other calculations you might want to perform on this worksheet, let's look at ways to format your information to make it easier to read at a glance. We'll show you how to make the results of your calculations stand out from your data and how to format the data itself so that it is neat and consistent. As your worksheets grow in complexity, you'll find that paying attention to such details will keep you oriented and help others understand your results.

Creating a Calculation Area

Usually when you create a worksheet, you are interested not so much in the individual pieces of information as in the results of the calculations you perform on the pieces. The worksheet you are working with now fits neatly on one screen, but often worksheets of this type include several screenfuls of information. It's a good idea to design your worksheets so that the important information is easily accessible, and it helps if this information is always in a predictable location. For these reasons, we leave room in the top-left corner of our worksheets for a calculation area. This habit is useful for the following reasons:

- We don't have to scroll around looking for totals and other results because we always know where to find them.

- We can print just the first page of the worksheet to get a report of the most pertinent information.

- We can easily jump to the calculation area from anywhere on the worksheet by pressing Ctrl-Home to move to cell A1.

Let's create an area at the top of the SALES.XLS worksheet for a title and a set of calculations. We'll start by freeing up some space at the top of the worksheet:

1. Select cells A1:E14, and use the Cut and Paste commands or Cell Drag And Drop editing to move the selection to A10:E23. Click OK when Excel asks whether you want to overwrite nonblank cells. (The nonblank cell you are overwriting is the SUM formula in cell E15.) Your screen now looks like this:

As you can see, Excel can handle overlapping cut and paste areas without garbling the results. Now let's enter the worksheet title:

2. Select A1, type *Preliminary Sales Analysis*, and press Enter.

3. With cell A2 selected, type *1st Quarter 1992*, and press Enter.

Next, we'll set off the calculation area. With Excel, you can get really fancy, using borders and shading to draw attention to calculation results. Later in this chapter, we show you some special techniques for formatting your worksheets. For now, though, let's draw lines of asterisks above and below the area, using one of Excel's special alignment formats.

1. With A3 selected, type one asterisk, and click the Enter box.   ← **Repeating characters**

2. Now select A3:E3, and choose the Alignment command from the Format menu. Excel displays this dialog box:

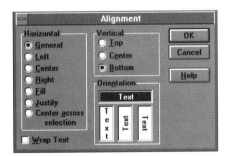

3. Select Fill, and click OK. The result is shown on the next page.

Other repeating characters

You can use the Fill option in the Alignment dialog box to repeat any character or group of characters so that they fill a single cell or a range of cells. Some common examples of other repeating characters are hyphens and equal signs. You might also want to experiment with combinations, such as hyphen-space-asterisk, to create different effects.

Flexible fill

Using the Fill option is more efficient than typing countless characters, not only because it saves typing time but also because the Fill option responds to changes you make to column widths. For example, if you decrease the width of column A, Excel adjusts the number of asterisks accordingly, so that they continue to fill the selected ranges.

Optical illusion

If you click the cells that appear to contain asterisks in columns B through E, you will see that they are empty. The only asterisk is the single one you typed in column A. If you enter another character in any of these cells, Excel repeats the character in that cell and in all cells to the right of it that have the Fill format.

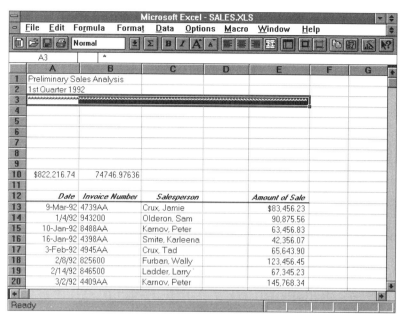

4. Press the Ctrl key, click the border of the selected range, and drag a copy of the row of asterisks down to the range A9:E9.

Now that we have created a calculation area, let's move the calculation in cell A10. Follow these steps:

1. Select A4, type *Total Sales*, and then click the Enter box.

2. Select A10, click its border, and drag its outline to B4.

3. Select B10, and use the Clear command to clear the cell.

4. Select A4:A8, and click the Bold tool on the toolbar. Here's the result:

Why did we tell you to select the empty cells below the Total Sales label before applying the bold format? Try this:

1. Select A5, and type *Average Sale*. The new label is bold, because we have already applied the bold format to cell A5.

2. Use any of the techniques you learned in Chapter 1 to widen column A so that you can see both the labels you have entered (refer to pages 30 and 31). From now on, adjust the column widths as necessary to see your work.

Formatting Text

In Chapter 1, you learned how to format entries by using tools on the toolbar to change alignment and make entries bold or italic. In this section, we'll get a bit more elaborate and show you how to change the font of the worksheet title and make the title bigger so that it really stands out. Here's how:

1. Select cell A1, and choose Font from either the Format menu or the shortcut menu. Excel displays this dialog box:

Changing fonts and sizes

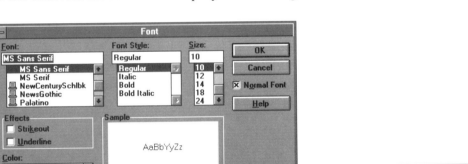

2. Select Roman in the Font list box, Bold in the Font Style list box, and 18 in the Size list box. Click OK. Notice that the height of row 1 increases to accommodate the larger font.

3. Select cell A2, and choose Font from the Format menu.

4. Select Roman in the Font list box, Bold Italic in the Font Style list box, and 14 in the Size list box. Click OK.

Now let's center the text over the calculation area using a new Excel 4 text alignment option.

The Font dialog box

The fonts listed in the Font dialog box depend on such factors as the resolution of your screen, which fonts were installed with Windows, which additional printer fonts are installed, and which version of Windows is installed.

You might want to use the display in the Sample section of the Font dialog box to experiment with combinations of font, size, and style before you apply a format to the selected cells.

1. Select A1:E2, and then click the Center Across Columns tool. As shown below, Excel centers the text over the selected area, but the labels remain in cells A1 and A2.

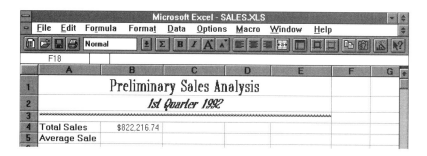

Displaying Dollars and Cents

Until you selected the table you created in Chapter 1 and formatted it using the AutoFormat tool, Excel displayed all numeric values you entered using the default General format. With this format, Excel simply displays what you typed (or what it thinks you typed), right-aligning the values without changing their appearance. However, Excel provides many formats that do change the way the values look. Try this:

Number formats →

1. Select cell E13, and choose Number from the Format menu. Excel displays this dialog box:

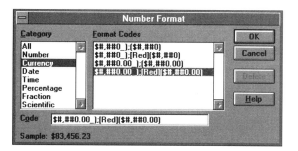

In the Category section of the dialog box, Excel highlights Currency. In the Format Codes list box, Excel displays the available currency formats and highlights a representation of the format applied to cell E13. The part of the format in front of the semicolon (;) is for positive numbers, and the part after the semicolon is for negative numbers. In this case, negative numbers will be displayed in parentheses (and in red on a color monitor, as indicated by the [RED] part of the code).

The format tells Excel to display a dollar sign ($) followed by the value (#,##0.00), using commas to group digits in threes. The # signs are placeholders for optional numbers, and the 0s are placeholders for numbers that Excel must display. Thus, Excel must display at least one digit to the left of the decimal point and two to the right. If the value is less than $1—for example, if it is 93 cents—Excel is to display $0.93, and if the value has no fractional part—for example, if it is exactly $1—Excel is to display $1.00. The Sample section of the dialog box shows how the entry in the active cell looks with the selected format.

The _) part of the format tells Excel to shift positive values away from the right border of the cell by the amount of space necessary to hold a closing parenthesis. As a result, in a column containing both negative and positive values, all the values will be decimal-aligned. To test this effect, try the following:

2. Click Cancel to close the dialog box.

3. Select cell B5, type *–$1,234.56*, and click the Enter box. Excel displays the value in parentheses, aligning the value with the positive value above it.

Now let's format the values in the Amount of Sale column as currency, this time copying the format from cell E13:

1. Select E13, and choose Copy from the Edit menu.

Alignment options

As you saw on page 45, choosing Alignment from the Format menu displays the Alignment dialog box, which enables you to align text in various ways. You can use the Wrap Text option to wrap text to multiple lines in a cell, rather than having it run into adjacent cells. Excel automatically adjusts the row height to accommodate all the text within the selected cell. The Center Across Selection option, which is similiar to the Center Across Columns tool, centers text in a selected range. You can use the Vertical alignment options to position text at the bottom, top, or center of a cell. (As with the Wrap Text option, Excel adjusts row height to accommodate all the text within a cell when you use the Vertical options.) You can use the Orientation options to run text vertically in a cell, either facing up, down, or with letters stacked on top of one another.

Preformatting for efficiency

Formatting blank cells is an efficient way to build a worksheet. For example, if you know that a block of cells will contain the dollar result of a formula, you can preformat the entire block.

2. Select the range E14:E23, and choose Paste Special from the Edit menu. In the Paste section of the dialog box, select Formats, and then click OK. Excel pastes the format from E13 into the selected cells, adding a dollar sign to the values.

Formatting Dates

In Chapter 1, we entered dates in column A in a variety of formats. Now we'll show you how to change the date format to reflect the needs of your worksheet. Let's experiment with the dates in column A:

1. Select A13:A23, and choose Number from either the Format menu or the shortcut menu.

2. In the Number Format dialog box, select Date from the Category list, select different formats from the Format Codes list, and look at the Sample section of the dialog box to see how the selected cells will appear with those formats. (Drag the dialog box out of the way if it blocks column A.)

3. Select the m/d/yy format, and click OK. Here's the result:

Entering in format

You can enter values "in format" instead of selecting a format from the Number Format dialog box. For example, if you enter $12,345 and then open the Number Format dialog box, Excel highlights the $#,##0_);($#,##0) format (currency with no decimal places), because it has enough information to preformat the entry. If you enter $12,345.67 instead, Excel recognizes that the value has the $#,##0.00_);($#,##0.00) format.

Using Styles

In Excel, you can group cell formats together in styles. Excel has six built-in styles that can quickly change the way cells look. The names of these six styles are displayed in the Style drop-down list box when you click the Style box on the Standard toolbar, as shown here:

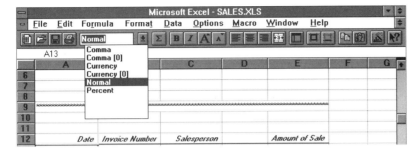

These six styles produce the following effects:

- The Normal style combines the General number format and the default font and size. However, you can add font, alignment, and other formats to define Normal to suit your needs. (See page 53 for information about defining styles.)

- The Comma style inserts commas to group digits in values greater than 999 into threes.

- The Comma [0] style formats numeric values the same way as the Comma style, but truncates the display of numbers to the right of the decimal point. Underlying values are unchanged.

- The Currency style adds a dollar sign in front of the value, uses commas to group digits by threes, and displays two decimal places (cents).

Quick styles

You don't need to open the Style dialog box to create a style. Simply apply all the formats you want to be part of the style, and highlight the current style name in the Style list. Then type a new name for the style, and press Enter. Excel adds the new style to the list. To redefine a style, follow the same steps, but press Enter instead of typing a new name. When Excel asks whether to redefine the style, click OK.

Sharing styles

You can share a style you create in one worksheet with another worksheet. Copy a cell formatted with the style, and paste it in the destination worksheet. The style travels with the copied cell. You can also use the Style dialog box to copy styles. Open both the source and the destination worksheets, and choose Style from the Format menu to display the Style dialog box. Click the Define button to expand the dialog box, and then click the Merge button. Select the source worksheet in the dialog box that appears, and click OK. Excel copies all the styles in the source worksheet to the destination worksheet.

• The Currency [0] style formats numbers the same way as the Currency style, but truncates the display of numbers to the right of the decimal point. Underlying values are unchanged.

• The Percent style displays the value as a percentage and appends a percent sign.

Applying a style from the Style list box is a simple matter of selecting the cell or range you want to format and then selecting the desired style from the list box. Try this:

Applying styles

1. Select E13:E23, and choose Currency [0] from the Style list. Excel reformats the range as shown here:

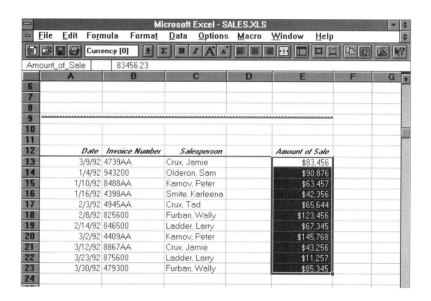

Direct dialog-box access

The buttons in the Change section of the expanded Style dialog box display the dialog boxes you see if you choose the corresponding command from the Format menu. For example, when defining a style, you can access the Alignment dialog box by choosing the Alignment command from the Format menu or by clicking the Alignment button in the expanded Style dialog box.

Underlying vs. displayed

After you apply a format, the value displayed in the cell might look different from the value in the formula bar. For example, 345.6789 might be displayed in its cell as $345.68 if you apply one of the currency formats. When performing calculations, Excel will use the value in the formula bar, called the underlying value, not the displayed value.

2. To return the numbers to their original state, choose Undo Style from the Edit menu.

In this case, applying a style did not produce dramatic results, but using styles can save you a lot of formatting time. For example, if you always format currency to be displayed in bold italics with two decimal places, you can create a style (or redefine one of Excel's built-in styles) that applies these formats. Try this:

1. Select E13:E23, and click the Bold and Italic tools.

2. Choose Style from the Format menu to display this dialog box:

Defining styles

3. In the Style Name text box, enter a name for the style—in this case, type *My Currency*. As soon as you start typing, the Description section of the Style dialog box changes to list all the formats in the selected cells.

4. Click OK. You return to the worksheet, where Excel has added My Currency to the Style list. You can now apply the new style to any cell by selecting the style from the Style list.

Custom formats

You can create your own formats or modify an existing format to meet special formatting needs. A detailed discussion of creating custom formats could take an entire chapter, but here are the basic steps for creating a numeric format: Start by entering a number in a cell, and choose Number from the Format menu or the shortcut menu. Select a format that resembles the one you want to create. (If none of the formats is similar to the one you want, clear the Format text box, and start from scratch.) Use 0s as required digit placeholders and #s as optional digit placeholders. Use @ as a text placeholder. Also enter any text that you want to be part of the format, enclosing the text in quotation marks. For example, if the value is 124 and you want Excel to display *You owe me $124.00* in the cell, you would create this format:

"You owe me " $##0.00

More Calculations

Now we'll move back to the calculation area and perform some more calculations on the sales data, starting with the average sale.

Averaging Values

The AVERAGE function

To find the average amount for the invoices we've entered in this worksheet, we'll use Excel's AVERAGE function. We'll also show you how to use the Paste Function command to avoid making errors while typing function names and to indicate the arguments Excel needs to calculate the function.

Pasting functions

1. Select cell B5, and choose Paste Function from the Formula menu. Excel displays this dialog box:

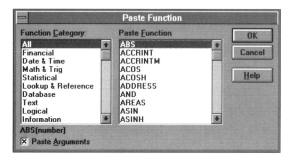

As with formats in the Number Format dialog box, Excel lists functions by category or in one big list if the All category is selected.

2. In the Paste Function list box, scroll to AVERAGE, and click to highlight it.

3. Check that the Paste Arguments option is selected, and then click OK. The formula bar now looks like this:

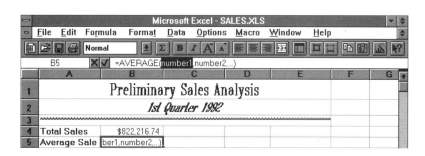

Notice that the *number1* argument is highlighted. To calculate the average of a series of numeric values, you could type the values in the formula bar in place of the argument names. In this example, you want to replace the first argument name with the reference of the range that contains the values you want to average and then delete the other arguments.

4. Select the range E13:E23 to replace *number1*. Then highlight *,number2,...* and press the Del key to delete the extra argument. The formula bar now looks like this:

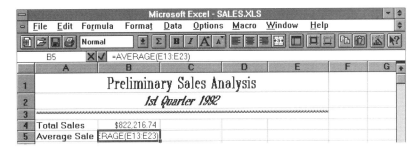

5. Click the Enter box to record the formula in cell B5. Excel displays the result: $74,746.98.

Identifying Highest and Lowest Sales

Excel provides two functions that instantly identify the highest and lowest values in a group. To understand the benefits of these functions, imagine that the SALES.XLS worksheet contains data from not 11 but 111 invoices! Let's start with the highest sale:

1. Select cell A6, type *Highest Sale*, and then press Tab to enter the text and select cell B6.

2. Choose Paste Function from the Formula menu, and highlight MAX in the Paste Function list box. (You can scroll to the function and select it, but a quicker way is to press M twice.)

The MAX function

3. This time, be sure that the Paste Arguments option is not selected so that you don't have to delete text from the formula bar. Then click OK. Excel pastes in only the function, with an insertion point between the open and close parentheses.

4. Select the range E13:E23, and click the Enter box. Excel enters the highest sale amount, $145,768.34, in cell B6.

Now for the formula for the lowest sale, which we'll type in the formula bar:

1. Select cell A7, type *Lowest Sale*, and press Tab.

The MIN function

2. Type *=MIN(E13:E23)*, and press Enter. Excel displays the result, $11,256.90, in cell A7.

Calculating with Names

The last calculation we'll make with this set of data involves the Total Sales value from cell B4. As a gross indicator of sales expenses, let's calculate the total sales commission:

1. First, insert a couple of new rows in the calculation area by clicking the headings for rows 8 and 9 and choosing Insert from either the Edit menu or the shortcut menu.

2. Select cell A8, type *Commission*, and press Tab.

3. Type *5%*, and click the Enter box.

4. With cell B8 still active, choose Define Name from the Formula menu. Excel scans the adjacent cells and suggests the name Commission. Click OK.

5. Select cell A9, type *Sales Expense*, and press Tab.

6. With cell B9 active, type *=Total*Commission*, and press Enter. Excel multiplies the value in the cell named Total (B4) by the value in the cell named Commission (B8) and displays the result, $41,110.84, in cell B9.

7. Now select cell B8, type *6%*, and press Enter. The value in cell B9 changes to reflect the new commission rate, as shown here:

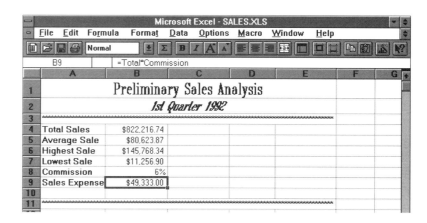

If a hundred calculations throughout the worksheet involved the name Commission, Excel would have adjusted all their results to reflect this one change.

Formulas That Make Decisions

There will be times when you want Excel to carry out one task under certain circumstances and another task if those circumstances don't apply. To give Excel this kind of instruction, you use the IF function.

Using the IF Function

In its simplest form, the IF function tests the value of a cell and does one thing if the test is positive (true) and another if the test is negative (false). It requires three arguments: the test, the action to perform if the test is true, and the action to perform if the test is false. You supply the arguments one after the other within the function's parentheses, separating them with commas (no spaces). Try this:

The IF function

1. Select D4, type the following, and then click the Enter box:

=IF(B4=0,"TRUE","FALSE")

Excel checks whether the value of B4 is zero (the test), and because it isn't, it bypasses TRUE (the action to perform if the test is true) and displays FALSE (the action to perform if the test is false) in cell D4.

2. With cell D4 still selected, highlight =0 in the formula bar, type *<1000000*, and click the Enter box. The entry in cell D4 instantly changes from FALSE to TRUE, because the value in cell B4 is less than one million (in other words, the test is true).

In this example, the test Excel performed was a simple evaluation of the value in a cell. However, you can also build tests that involve other functions. Recall that the last two characters of the invoice numbers in column B of the worksheet indicate whether the sale originated in your company's East or West office. Suppose you want to assign East and West entries to each invoice so that you can compare the performance of the two offices. Follow the steps on the next page to experiment with a more complex IF example.

Functions in tests

1. Select cell D14, type *Office*, and press Enter. Excel displays the label in bold italics, because the formats from the old column D were applied to the new column D when you inserted it.

2. In cell D15, type the following, and click the Enter box:

The RIGHT function →

=IF(RIGHT(B15,2)="AA","East","West")

You have told Excel to look at the two characters at the right end of the value in cell B15 and, if they are AA, to enter East in cell D15. If they are not AA, Excel is to enter West. Here's the result:

Using Nested IF Functions

When constructing tests, you can use IF functions within IF functions. Called nested functions, these formulas add another dimension to the complexity of the decisions Excel can make. Here's a quick demonstration:

1. Insert a new column between columns A and B, and enter the column label *Quarter* in cell B14.

2. Select B15:B25, and choose Number from the Format menu. Then select All from the Category list and General from the Format Codes list, and click OK.

Logical operators

Here is a list of operators you can use with the IF function:

= < > <> >= <=

You can also use AND and OR to combine two or more tests. The function

=IF(AND(B4=0,B5>0),"Yes","No")

displays Yes only if both tests are true. The function

=IF(OR(B4=0,B5>0),"Yes","No")

displays Yes if either test is true.

3. Select cell B15 in the new column, and type the following on one line:

```
=IF(MONTH(A15)<4,1,IF(MONTH(A15)<7,2,
    IF(MONTH(A15)<10,3,4)))
```

The MONTH function

4. Check your typing, paying special attention to all the parentheses, and then click the Enter box.

You have told Excel to check the month component of the date in cell A15. If it is less than 4, Excel is to display 1 in the corresponding cell in the Quarter column. If the month is not less than 4 but is less than 7, Excel is to display 2 in the Quarter column. If it is not less than 7 but is less than 10, Excel is to display 3. Otherwise, Excel is to display 4. If you have typed the formula correctly, Excel enters 1 in cell B15.

Copying Formulas

The IF functions you have just entered are pretty arduous to type, even for good typists. Fortunately, you don't have to enter them more than once. With the Fill Down command on the Edit menu, you can copy the formulas into other cells. Here's how:

1. Select B15:B25, and choose Fill Down from the Edit menu.

Copying down a range

Another, easier way to fill a range with a formula is to use the AutoFill feature, which is part of Cell Drag And Drop editing. Follow these steps:

1. Select cell E15, and position the pointer over the small black square in the bottom-right corner of the cell. The pointer changes to a dark cross hair called the AutoFill pointer.

2. Click, and drag down to cell E25. The worksheet now looks like the one on the next page.

Text values as arguments

When entering text values as arguments in a formula, you must enclose them in quotation marks. Otherwise Excel thinks the text is a name and returns the #NAME? error value in the cell.

3. Select cell E15, and look at the formula in the formula bar. Excel has changed the original formula

=IF(RIGHT(B15,2)="AA","East","West")

to

=IF(RIGHT(C15,2)="AA","East","West")

Excel changed the reference to account for the addition of the Quarter column. If you click cell E16, you'll see that when you used Fill Down, Excel changed the reference so that it refers to cell C16, not cell C15.

Relative references

By default, Excel uses relative references in its formulas. Relative references refer to cells by their position in relation to the cell containing the formula. So when you copied the formula in cell E15 to cell E16, Excel changed the reference in the formula from C15 to C16—the cell in the same row and two columns to the left of the cell containing the formula. If you were to copy the formula in cell E15 to F15, Excel would change the reference from C15 to D15 so that the formula would continue to reference the cell in the same relative position.

Absolute references

When you don't want a reference to be copied as a relative reference, as it was in the preceding examples, you need to use an absolute reference. Absolute references refer to cells by their fixed position in the worksheet. To make a reference absolute, you add dollar signs before its column letter and row number. For example, to change the reference C4:C9 to an absolute reference, you would enter it as $C$4:$C$9. You could then move a formula that contained this reference anywhere on the worksheet, and it would always refer to the range C4:C9.

References can also be partially relative and partially absolute. For example, $C3 has an absolute column reference and a relative row reference, and C$3 has a relative column reference and an absolute row reference.

Printing Your Worksheets

If your primary purpose in learning Excel is to be able to manipulate your own information and come up with results that will guide your decision-making, your worksheets might never need to leave your computer. If, on the other hand, you want to sway the decisions of your colleagues or you need to prepare reports for your board of directors, you will probably need printed copies of your worksheets. Now is a good time to cover how to preview and print an Excel document.

Print Preview

Usually, you will want to preview your worksheets before you print them to make sure that single-page documents fit neatly on the page and that multi-page documents break in logical places. You can use Zoom view (see tip) to give you an idea of how your worksheet is structured, but it won't give you a real feel for how your document will look when printed. This is where Print Preview comes in handy. In Print Preview, you can change margins, column widths, and the basic page layout, but you cannot make any modifications to the values in the worksheet. Let's preview SALES.XLS:

1. Choose Print Preview from the File menu. The Print Preview window opens, with a miniature version of the printed worksheet displayed, as shown on the next page.

Zoom view

A new feature in Excel 4 is the ability to zoom in and out of areas of a worksheet. After choosing Zoom from the Window menu, you can select a magnification of anywhere from 10% to 400%. Although the larger magnifications might be useful for users with impaired vision, you are more likely to want to zoom out to get an overview of your worksheet's structure.

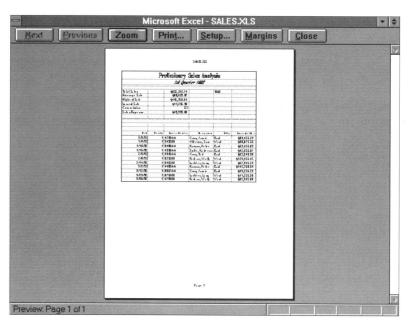

Notice that Excel will print only the rectangular block needed to hold all the cells containing entries.

2. Move the mouse pointer over the page. The pointer changes to a small magnifying glass.

Zooming in and out

3. To examine part of the page in more detail, move the magnifying glass over that part, and click the mouse button. Excel zooms in on that portion of the page. Click again to zoom out (or click the Zoom button at the top of the screen).

Setting Up the Pages

By default, Excel prints your worksheet with gridlines around each cell, the worksheet's filename as a header at the top of the page, and a page number as a footer at the bottom of the page. For presentation purposes, these default settings don't produce a very attractive printout, so you'll probably want to change them. You make these changes in the Page Setup dialog box, which Excel displays when you choose Page Setup from the File menu. When you are in Print Preview, you can also access this dialog box directly.

Printer setup

If your computer can access more than one printer, or if you need to set up the printer to print with Excel, click the Printer Setup button in the Page Setup dialog box, and select the printer you want to use or adjust. Then make the necessary settings in each printer's setup dialog box before trying to print. Any changes you make in these dialog boxes remain in effect for printing in all Windows applications.

1. Click the Setup button at the top of the Print Preview window to display a Page Setup dialog box something like this one:

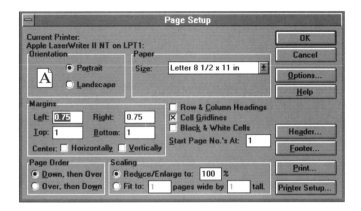

(Your dialog box might differ slightly, depending on the type of printer you have.)

2. Click the Header button to display the Header dialog box. You use the Header and Footer dialog boxes to add, delete, and edit headers and footers. To add a header, you enter text and codes in the appropriate boxes and click the buttons in the middle of the dialog box.

Creating headers

3. Highlight &F in the Center Section box, and type *&bSales Analysis*. The &b code tells Excel to print the text in bold.

4. Click OK to return to the Page Setup dialog box, and then click Footer to open the Footer dialog box. The default footer is displayed in the Center Section box, indicating that the footer will also be centered. The word *Page* followed by the &P code instructs Excel to print the word *Page* followed by the page number as the footer.

Creating footers

Header and footer codes

The buttons in the Header and the Footer dialog boxes add codes that do the following:

&P	Adds current page number
&N	Inserts total number of pages
&D	Adds current date
&T	Adds current time
&F	Adds filename

Here are some other codes:

&B	Prints following codes in bold
&I	Italicizes following characters
&U	Underlines following characters

5. Highlight Page &P, and press Del to delete it. Then click OK. Excel returns to the Page Setup dialog box.

Page centering

Turning off gridlines

6. Click Center Horizontally and Center Vertically to center the worksheet horizontally and vertically on the page. Then click Cell Gridlines to turn it off, and click OK. You return to the Print Preview window, which now looks like this:

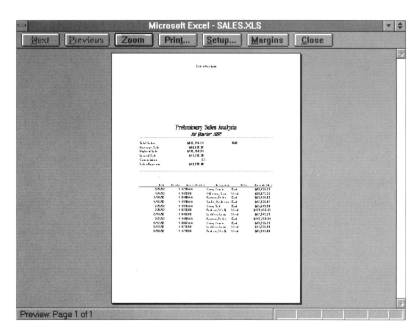

Adjusting margins and column widths

You can adjust the margins and column widths of your printout in the Print Preview window by clicking the Margins button to display guidelines and then manually moving the guidelines to increase or decrease the margins and columns.

Setting page breaks

If you want to print the calculation area on one page and the supporting data on another, or if you need to control where the pages break in a multi-page worksheet, select the cell below the row and to the right of the column at which you want Excel to break the page, and choose Set Page Break from the Options menu.

Removing page breaks

To remove a manual page break, select the cell immediately below and to the right of the page break, and choose Remove Page Break from the Options menu. Or select the entire document by clicking the square that appears at the top-left corner of the worksheet (at the intersection of the row and column headings), and then choose Remove Page Break. All page breaks in the worksheet will be removed.

Repeating labels

To repeat row or column labels on all pages of a multi-page worksheet, highlight the entire rows and columns containing the labels, and choose Set Print Titles from the Options menu. In the Set Print Titles dialog box, accept the default options, and click OK. Then select all the cells of the worksheet below the labels, and choose Set Print Area from the Options menu.

If you need to return to the worksheet to make additional changes before printing, you can close the Print Preview window by clicking the Close button.

Getting Ready to Print

When you are ready to print, you can simply choose the Print command from the File menu or click the Print tool if you are in the regular document window, or you can print directly from the Print Preview window by following these steps:

1. Click the Print button in the Print Preview window. Excel displays the Print dialog box for your printer. (This dialog box is also displayed when you choose Print from the File menu, but not when you click the Print tool.) Here's an example of this dialog box for a PostScript printer:

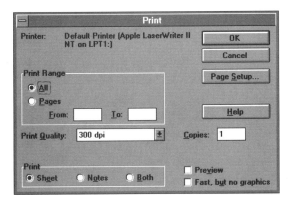

Because the Print dialog box varies for different printers, we'll keep our instructions here very general.

2. In the Copies text box, enter the number of copies to print. *Number of copies*

3. To print the entire worksheet, leave the Print Range option set to All. Otherwise, indicate the desired pages in the Pages From and Pages To text boxes. *Page range*

4. Check that the Preview option is not selected. (Selecting this option is another way to display the Print Preview window.)

5. Check that your printer is ready to go, and then click OK.

6. After looking at your printed worksheet, save it again.

   That should do it. We've done a lot of work in this chapter, and you can now evaluate the results on paper.

3

Extracting Information from a Database

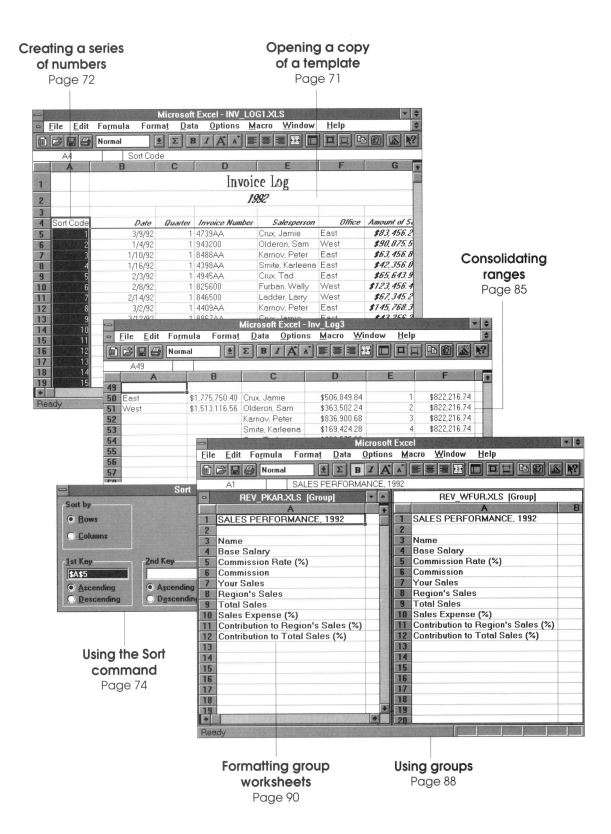

Creating a series of numbers
Page 72

Opening a copy of a template
Page 71

Consolidating ranges
Page 85

Using the Sort command
Page 74

Formatting group worksheets
Page 90

Using groups
Page 88

To work efficiently with Excel takes more than just learning how to input and format data. By simply planning ahead and putting to use some tried-and-true tricks and time-saving techniques, you can save yourself hours of tedious work at the computer. That's why we think it is important now to show you how to clone worksheets (use one worksheet as the foundation for building another), create reusable templates, sort and extract data, and link worksheets so that when you update one, all are updated. Where to begin? Let's start by creating an invoice log.

Cloning Worksheets

Using one worksheet as the basis for another is an important time-saving technique. In this section, we will clone the SALES.XLS worksheet to create another worksheet called INV_LOG.XLS. Then we'll use a few tricks to transform the new worksheet into a simulated invoice log (a record of sales). If you need to create such a log for your work, you can key in real data. In Chapter 6, we show you how to automate the process of inputting this kind of information so that you are spared hours of typing. In the meantime, though, let's create a simulated log to give us a large worksheet to manipulate in the other sections of this chapter. Follow these steps to create INV_LOG.XLS:

Duplicating worksheets

1. Click the Open File tool on the Standard toolbar, and locate and open SALES.XLS.

2. Delete the extraneous formula in cell E4, and choose Save As from the File menu.

3. In the File Name text box, type *inv_log*, and click OK.

   You now have two nearly identical worksheets saved under different names. A few alterations to INV_LOG.XLS will give you a useable sample worksheet.

1. Select A1, type *Invoice Log*, and press Enter to both enter the text and select cell A2. Then type *1992*, and press Enter. Notice that both entries retain the text formatting of the previous entries and are centered over the table.

2. Select the headings for rows 3 through 12, and choose Delete from the shortcut menu.

3. Select A5:F15, and choose Copy from the shortcut menu.

4. Choose Insert Paste from the shortcut menu, select the Shift Cells Down option, and click OK.

5. Select A5:F26, copy the range, and repeat step 4 to create a log containing 44 invoices.

Now, so that the log includes invoices for all the months of the year, follow these steps:

1. Select A16. Highlight 3 (the month) in the formula bar, type *4*, and press Enter. Excel displays the new date for this invoice and then recalculates the formula in cell B16, assigning the invoice to the second quarter of the year instead of the first.

Rather than changing dates manually for the rest of the work-sheet, we'll take this opportunity to demonstrate the Series command on the Data menu. Later in this chapter, we'll use this command to create a sequential set of numbers. Here, we'll use it to create a set of evenly spaced dates. (If you were logging real invoices in this database, you would use the actual sale dates.)

2. Select A16:A26, and choose the Series command from the Data menu. Excel displays this dialog box:

Creating a series of dates

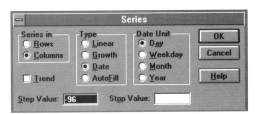

3. Because the value in cell A16 is a date, Excel assumes you want to create a set of dates. Click the Weekday option, type *4* in the Step Value box, and then click OK. Excel uses the value in cell A16 as its starting point and creates a series of dates that are four business days apart, skipping to Monday if a date falls on Saturday or Sunday.

Calculating dates using weekdays

4. Select cell A27, highlight 3 in the formula bar, type *7*, and press Enter.

5. Select A27:A37, and choose Repeat Series from the Edit menu.

6. Select cell A38, highlight 3 in the formula bar, type *10*, and press Enter.

7. Select A38:A48, and choose Repeat Series from the Edit menu.

Notice that your worksheet now contains invoices for all four quarters of the year. The formulas in column B have done their work and assigned the invoices to quarters based on the dates in column A.

This large worksheet is ideal for demonstrating some of Excel's database features, but before we launch to that topic, we'll show you how to convert INV_LOG.XLS to a template that you can use as a basis for several worksheets.

Creating Templates

Worksheet ideas

Invoice logs like the one you just created can be used as the basis for many kinds of worksheets. For example, you might want to analyze sales by quarter to detect seasonal trends, sales by regional office to determine management effectiveness, and sales by person to evaluate individual performance. If you include product information in your log, you can also evaluate product performance and the contribution of each product to the company's bottom line. To perform any of these analyses, you use a copy of the invoice log, not the log itself, because you want the original log to remain intact as a permanent record.

Excel allows you to designate worksheets as templates that you can use over and over again. When you select a template as the worksheet you want to open, Excel opens a copy of the template, not the template itself, using the template name followed by a number as the worksheet name.

Let's save INV_LOG.XLS as a template now. Here's how:

Saving a template

1. Choose Save As from the File menu, and then click the arrow to the right of the Save File As Type text box to display a drop-down list of the formats in which you can save a worksheet.

2. Select Template. Notice that Excel changes the extension in the File Name text box from XLS to XLT to designate the file as an Excel template. Click OK to save the template with the name INV_LOG.XLT.

3. Now choose Close from the File menu to close the template.

4. Pull down the File menu, and choose INV_LOG.XLT from the list of recently opened files. Excel opens a copy of the template with the name Inv_Log1, as shown here:

Opening a copy of a template

	A	B	C	D	E	F
1		Invoice Log				
2		1992				
3						
4	Date	Quarter	Invoice Number	Salesperson	Office	Amount of Sale
5	3/9/92	1	4739AA	Crux, Jamie	East	$83,456.23
6	1/4/92	1	943200	Olderon, Sam	West	$90,875.56
7	1/10/92	1	8488AA	Karnov, Peter	East	$63,456.83
8	1/16/92	1	4398AA	Smite, Karleena	East	$42,356.07
9	2/3/92	1	4945AA	Crux, Tad	East	$65,643.90
10	2/8/92	1	825600	Furban, Wally	West	$123,456.45
11	2/14/92	1	846500	Ladder, Larry	West	$67,345.23
12	3/2/92	1	4409AA	Karnov, Peter	East	$145,768.34
13	3/12/92	1	8867AA	Crux, Jamie	East	$43,256.23
14	3/23/92	1	875600	Ladder, Larry	West	$11,256.90
15	3/30/92	1	479300	Furban, Wally	West	$85,345.00
16	4/9/92	2	4739AA	Crux, Jamie	East	$83,456.23
17	4/15/92	2	943200	Olderon, Sam	West	$90,875.56
18	4/21/92	2	8488AA	Karnov, Peter	East	$63,456.83
19	4/27/92	2	4398AA	Smite, Karleena	East	$42,356.07

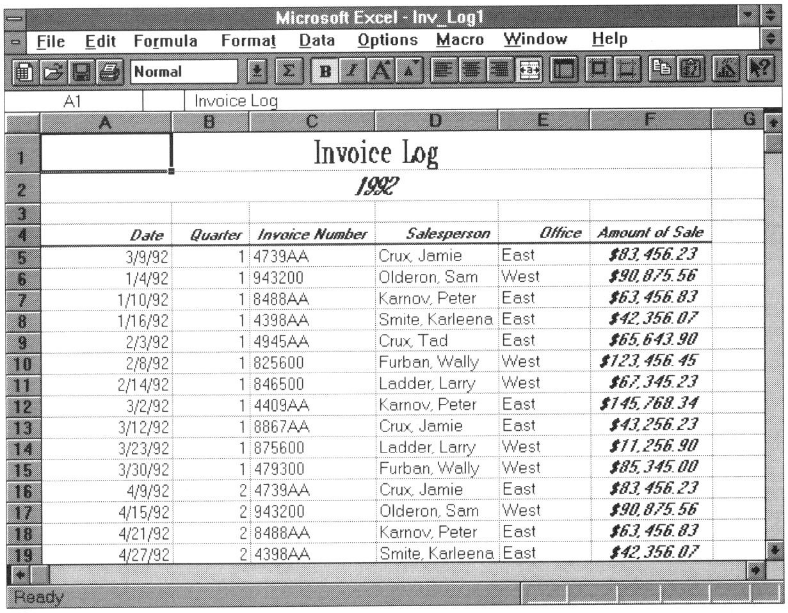

The XLSTART directory

When you first installed Excel, the installation program created a subdirectory called XLSTART in the Excel directory. Any worksheet, chart, or macro sheet you place in this directory will be opened when you start Excel. This directory is especially handy if you frequently use the same set of macros.

By default, when you choose the New command from the File menu, you can create new worksheets, charts, macro sheets, workbooks, and slides. In addition, if you save a document as a template in the XLSTART directory, the template will be listed in the New dialog box the next time you choose the New command. Selecting the template and clicking OK opens a copy of the template.

Editing templates

To make changes to the original template, open a copy of the template, make the changes, and save the new version in Template format with the same name as the original, thereby overwriting it.

5. Click the Save File tool on the toolbar. Excel then suggests that you save the copy of the template with the name INV_LOG1.XLS. Press Enter or click OK to accept this name.

Sorting Data

The sales data in the worksheet you created in Chapter 2 fits neatly on one screen. To find out which salesperson from the West office has made the highest single sale, you could simply look at the worksheet. Getting that information from the worksheet now on your screen is a little more difficult. Fortunately, Excel can quickly sort worksheets like this one, using one, two, or even three levels of sorting.

Adding Sort Codes

Before you sort any large worksheet, you should ask yourself whether you might need to put the data back in its original order. If there is even a chance that you will, you should add sort codes to the worksheet before you begin sorting. A sort code is a sequential number assigned to each row of entries. After sorting the entries, you can sort one more time on the basis of the sort code to put everything back where it was. Follow these steps to add sort codes to INV_LOG1.XLS:

Creating a series of numbers

1. Insert a blank column in front of the Date column by clicking the column A heading and choosing Insert from the shortcut menu.

2. Select cell A4, type *Sort Code*, and press Enter.

3. In cell A5, type *1*, and press Enter.

4. Select A5:A48, and choose Series from the Data menu.

5. The default settings—Columns as the Series In option, Linear as the Type option, and a Step Value of 1—will produce the result you want, so click OK. Excel uses the value in cell A5 as its starting point and inserts a sequential set of numbers in the selected range, as shown here:

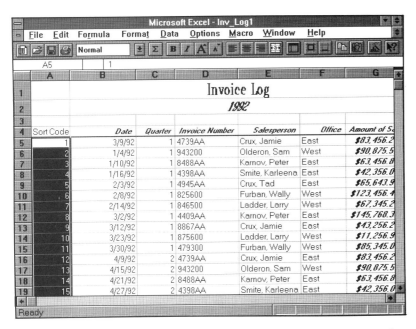

Now let's look at various ways you might want to sort the INV_LOG1.XLS worksheet.

Using One Sort Key

The simplest sorting procedure is based on only one set of criteria, or *sort key*. You indicate which column or row Excel should use, and the program rearranges the selected range accordingly. Follow the steps on the next page to sort the data in INV_LOG1.XLS by regional office so that you can see how the process works.

Automatic date series

You can use AutoFill to create a series of dates. Simply make your first entry—March, 1st Qtr, Monday, and so on—and then drag the AutoFill pointer through the range you want to fill. Excel assumes that you want to create a series with a step value of 1 (one month, quarter, day, and so on). To fill a range with the same date, without creating a series, hold down Ctrl while dragging the AutoFill pointer.

Automatic number series

To create a number series using AutoFill, follow the steps for creating a date series but enter a step value in the cell below the starting value so that Excel knows what to use as a step value. Then select both values, and drag the AutoFill pointer to create the series. If you don't enter the step value, Excel simply fills the range with the starting value.

1. Select A5:G48. (Remember, a quick way to select large ranges is to use the Goto command on the Formula menu. Enter the range reference in the Reference text box, and click OK to select the range.)

2. Choose Sort from the Data menu. Excel displays the Sort dialog box:

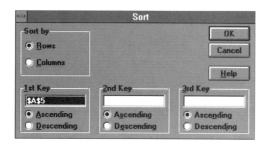

3. In the 1st Key text box, you need to designate the column you want Excel to use as the basis for the sort. Move the dialog box out of the way by dragging its title bar, and click any cell in column F. That cell's absolute reference replaces $A$5 (the active cell of the selected range) in the 1st Key text box.

4. Leave the Sort By option set to Rows and the sort order set to Ascending, and click OK. Here are the results:

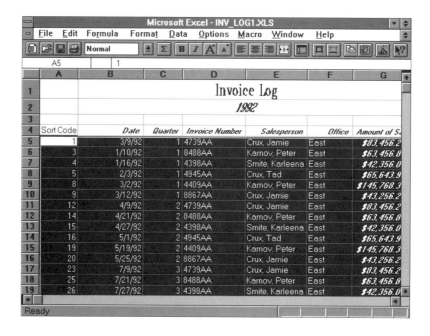

The invoice data is now sorted alphabetically by regional office, with all the invoices for the East office coming before those for the West office. As you can see if you look at the sort codes in column A, within the sorted regions the rows have stayed in numeric order.

Using Two Sort Keys

Now let's take things a step further and sort the invoices not only by regional office but also by salesperson.

1. With A5:G48 selected, choose Sort from the Data menu.

2. When Excel displays the Sort dialog box, again select a cell in column F for the 1st Key. Then click the 2nd Key text box, select a cell in column E, and click OK.

   The table is now sorted alphabetically by regional office and alphabetically within region by salesperson.

Using Three Sort Keys

Depending on the focus of your current analysis, you might want to sort INV_LOG1.XLS based on the Date or Quarter columns. However, let's assume you are interested in each person's sales performance and add one more key criteria to the sort. To sort by regional office, salesperson, and amount of sale, follow these steps:

1. With A5:G48 still selected, choose Sort from the Data menu.

Don't include labels

If you include row 4 in the range to be sorted, Excel sorts the column labels along with the entries. As a result, the labels might end up in the middle of the worksheet.

Sorting by columns

If your worksheet has labels down the leftmost column instead of across the top row and your data is oriented horizontally instead of vertically, you will want to sort by columns instead of rows.

Ascending vs. descending order

Ascending order places numbers before text, 1 before 2, and A before B. Descending order, on the other hand, does just the opposite. It places text before numbers, B before A, and 2 before 1.

2. Select a cell in column F for the 1st Key, and select a cell in column E for the 2nd Key. Then click the 3rd Key text box, select a cell in column G, and click OK.

Now you can easily spot the highest sales of each salesperson in both regions:

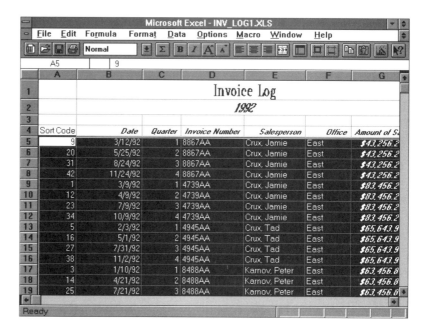

Freezing Labels

As you scroll through the invoice log to check how Excel has sorted the data, you'll probably find yourself wishing that the

Saving while sorting

Remember to save your worksheet often, perhaps after each sort. You can use Save As to create a new worksheet if you don't want to overwrite the results of one sort with the next. If you have activated the Autosave add-in macro, Excel saves changes automatically at timed intervals that you set.

Sort-key default

Excel does not retain sort-key settings from one sort to the next. When you choose the Sort command, the 1st Key text box reflects the active cell of the selected range. You must select the sort keys for every sort.

More than three keys

To sort a range on more than three fields, do multiple sorts. For example, to sort on five fields, first sort with the fifth, or least important, field in the 2nd Key text box and the fourth field in the 1st Key text box. Then sort with the third field in the 3rd Key text box, the second field in the 2nd Key text box, and the most important field in the 1st Key text box.

column labels hadn't scrolled out of sight. You can freeze the labels at the top of the screen by splitting the document window into two panes: one containing the labels and the other containing the data. Follow these steps to split the INV_LOG1.XLS window horizontally:

1. Scroll the worksheet so that row 4—the row with the column labels—is at the top of your screen.

2. Move the mouse pointer to the black bar, called the split bar, at the top of the right scroll bar.

Splitting windows into panes

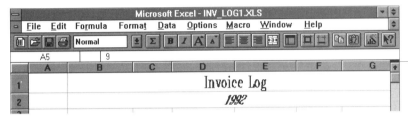

Split bar

When the pointer changes into a set of arrows, drag the split bar down between rows 4 and 5. Here's the result so far:

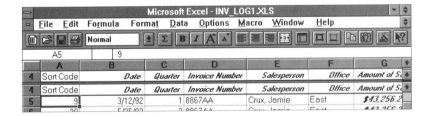

Synchronized scrolling

If you split the worksheet window horizontally and use the bottom scroll bar to scroll the window, both panes of the window scroll so that columns always align. Likewise, if you split the worksheet window vertically, using the right scroll bar scrolls the rows simultaneously.

The Split command

Using the Split command on the Window menu, you can split the worksheet window both vertically and horizontally at the same time. After you choose the command, you can use the split bars to reposition the split if necessary.

Freezing panes

You use the Freeze Panes command on the Window menu to lock the top, left, or top-left pane of a split window. You can then keep column or row headings in view while you scroll to other portions of the worksheet. The top and left scroll bars are unavailable when panes are frozen. Choose Unfreeze Panes to unfreeze the frozen windowpanes.

3. Use the scroll bar for the lower windowpane to scroll the sorted data while the column labels remain visible in the upper windowpane.

Closing split panes

4. When you finish viewing the data, restore the single pane by dragging the split bar back up to its original position at the top of the right scroll bar, or by double-clicking the split bar.

Next, we'll cover Excel's database capabilities. To see how easy it is to perform different kinds of manipulations on different versions of a template, let's save INV_LOG1.XLS in its current state and open a new copy of the template for use in the next section:

1. Save and close INV_LOG1.XLS.

2. Choose INV_LOG.XLT from the bottom of the File menu. Excel opens Inv_Log2 on your screen.

3. Save this copy of the template with the suggested name: INV_LOG2.XLS.

Database Basics

The invoice log is an organized collection of information about invoices. By common definition, it is a database.

A database is a table of related data with a rigid structure that enables you to easily locate and evaluate individual items of information. Each row of a database is a record that contains all the pertinent information about one component of the database. For example, row 5 of the invoice log contains all the information about one particular invoice. Each cell of the database is a field that contains one item of information. For example, cell F5 contains the amount of the invoice for the record in row 5. All the fields in a particular column contain the same kind of information about their respective records. For example, column G of the invoice log contains the amounts of all the invoices. At the top of each column is a label, called the field name.

Although the invoice log is a database by common definition, Excel does not yet recognize it as a database. Here's how you tell Excel that the log is a database:

1. Select A4:F49 using the Goto command on the Formula menu.

2. Choose Set Database from the Data menu.

Creating a database

That's it. After you specifically designate the range A4:F49 as a database, you can use commands on the Data menu to pull records that meet specific criteria out of the database for further examination or manipulation.

Manipulating Records

Suppose you invested a considerable chunk of your advertising budget for the year on a direct-mail flyer about a two-week promotion. For another two-week promotion earlier in the year, you relied on your salespeople to get the word out to their customers. You want to compare sales during the two promotions. Or suppose you want to analyze all sales over $60,000 to see if you can detect sales patterns. In either case, you can tell Excel to extract all the relevant invoices for scrutiny.

Database ideas

You give Excel instructions of this kind by defining criteria in an area of the worksheet called the criteria range. For example, you might tell Excel to find all the records with amounts over $60,000 by entering *>60000* in the criteria range under the Amount of Sale field name.

Mandatory field names

You must include the field names in the database range. If you neglect to include them, Excel will be unable to perform the Extract, Find, or Delete commands.

Field-naming conventions

Excel has several rules concerning field names in databases. No two field names can be the same. Also, field names cannot begin with a numeric value and cannot be blank. If they are, Excel will display an error message during database operations.

Creating the Criteria Range

As with worksheet calculation areas, it's a good idea to locate the criteria range at the top of the worksheet so that it is easy to get to from anywhere in the database. Let's insert a block of four rows above the database to use as a criteria range.

1. Select the headings for rows 4 through 7.

2. Choose Insert from the shortcut menu. Excel inserts the same number of rows you selected.

The top row of the criteria range always contains the field names of the fields you want to use as criteria for locating records, so start by copying the field names from the database to the criteria range:

1. Select A8:F8, and choose Copy from the shortcut menu.

2. Select A4, and choose Paste from the shortcut menu.

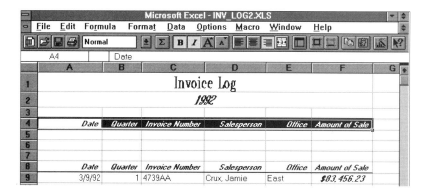

Only one database

Although you can build several tables of information on the same worksheet, only one of them can be designated as the active database at any given time. When you choose Set Database, Excel assigns the name Database to the selected range. Setting a different database assigns the name Database to the new range.

Adding records

When setting the database, always include at least one blank row at the bottom of the selected range. Then if you need to add records to the database, you can simply select the blank row and insert a new row to extend the database, instead of having to redefine the database.

Data forms

After you have set the database, you can use the Form command on the Data menu to open a dialog box that displays the first record of the database. Field names are shown on the left, and records are displayed in text boxes on the right. You can edit any field except those derived from formulas. Use the scroll bar to scroll through the records, and click the buttons in the dialog box to delete, create, and find records.

Now you need to set the criteria range so that Excel knows where in the database to look for the criteria. Here's how:

1. Select A4:F5, a range that includes the field names and the blank row beneath them where you will enter your criteria.

Setting the criteria range

2. Choose Set Criteria from the Data menu.

Entering Criteria

To have Excel locate specific records, you enter one or more criteria under the field names in the criteria range. For example, to locate all the invoices for Peter Karnov, you simply enter *Karnov, Peter* under the Salesperson field name in the criteria range. To locate invoices that are both for Peter Karnov *and* have amounts over $100,000—Excel is to locate records that meet both criteria—you enter *Karnov, Peter* under Salesperson, and *>100000* in the same row under Amount of Sale. To locate the invoices for Peter Karnov *or* Wally Furban—Excel is to locate records that meet either of the two criteria—you enter *Karnov, Peter* under the Salesperson field name in the first row and *Furban, Wally* under the Salesperson field name in the next row. (You then need to reset the criteria range to include the second row.)

Let's try entering criteria that will locate invoices for Peter Karnov that amount to more than $100,000:

1. In cell D5, type *Karnov, Peter*, and press Enter.

Using all field names

Technically, you can enter only the names of the fields you use as criteria in the criteria range. However, copying all the field names into your criteria range allows you to mix and match criteria as necessary, without having to erase and type the field names each time.

Only one criteria range

Only one range can be designated as the criteria range at any given time. When you choose the Set Criteria command, Excel assigns the name Criteria to the range you selected. Setting a different criteria range assigns the name Criteria to the new range.

No blank rows

You must enter some criteria in the criteria range before choosing the Find or Delete command from the Data menu. If you don't, Excel selects all the records, because the blank row does not specify any particular criteria. The presence of blank rows in the criteria range is particularly dangerous when you use the Delete command, because all records will be deleted.

2. In cell F5, type *>100000*, and press Enter.

You must now choose a command from the Data menu to tell Excel what to do with the records that match the criteria. Three commands are available: Find, Delete, and Extract.

Finding and Deleting Records

Choosing Find from the Data menu tells Excel to find and highlight the first record in the database that meets the criteria you entered in the criteria range. Let's try this now:

Finding records

1. Choose Find from the Data menu. Excel enters Find mode (indicated by the striped pattern in the scroll bars) and stops at this record:

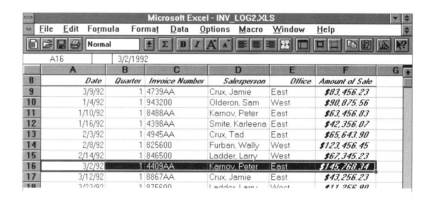

Comparison operators

You can use these comparison operators to compute criteria:

= > < >= <= <>

and you can specify wildcards, using the standard DOS wildcards * and ? for matching text. For example, specifying *Crux.** under Salesperson would locate the records for both Jamie Crux and Tad Crux.

Criteria in same field

If you want to locate records using two criteria in the same field, you must add a second field with the same field name to the criteria range. For example, to locate invoices that are dated after June 30 and before July 15, you would add a second Date field name, either in cell G4 or adjacent to the existing Date field name in cell A4, reset the criteria range, and enter *>6/30/912* under one Date field name and *<7/15/92* under the other Date field name.

2. Click the arrows at the bottom and top of the right scroll bar to move to the next and previous records that meet the criteria. (You can also press the Down and Up Arrow keys.)

3. Choose the Exit Find command from the Data menu or press Esc to leave Find mode.

Leaving Find mode

Choosing Delete from the Data menu tells Excel to find and delete the records that meet the criteria in the criteria range. When you choose this command, Excel displays a message box to warn you that the matching records will be permanently deleted. Click OK to proceed with the deletion, or click Cancel if you first want to check that the criteria you have entered won't cause Excel to delete records you really need to keep.

Deleting records

Extracting Records

Choosing Extract from the Data menu tells Excel to find and copy the records that meet the criteria into an area of the worksheet called the extract range. Before choosing this command, you must set the extract range so that Excel knows where to put the records. The procedure for creating the extract range is almost identical to the procedure for creating the criteria range, except that we always locate the extract range to the right of, or below, all existing worksheet entries so that there is no chance that extracted records will overwrite valuable information. Follow these steps to create an extract range in INV_LOG2.XLS:

1. Select A8:F8 (the field-name cells), and choose Copy from the shortcut menu.

2. Select H4, and choose Paste from the shortcut menu.

3. To widen the columns to fit the labels, choose Column Width from the Format menu, and click the Best Fit button. Then widen the Date and Salesperson columns slightly so that those entries will fit.

4. To allocate space for the extracted records, select H4:M4, and choose Set Extract from the Data menu. You can include cells below the field names in the extract range, but selecting a

Setting the extract range

range limits the number of records Excel can extract to the size of the range.

Now you can tell Excel to extract the records that meet the criteria in the criteria range:

1. Choose Extract from the Data menu. Excel displays this dialog box:

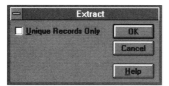

2. Click OK to start the extraction. Here's the result:

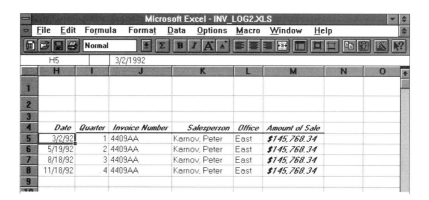

This discussion of databases has necessarily been brief, but you should now know enough to explore various ways of

---

Extract-range field names

As with the criteria range, the top row of the extract range must contain field names. If you include only some of the fields, Excel extracts only those fields from the database.

Extracting unique records

Using the Unique Records Only option in the Extract dialog box tells Excel to extract only one instance of repeated records. Because we repeated many records to create our database, selecting this option would result in fewer records in our extract range.

Preserving extracted records

When you extract records, Excel overwrites any previously extracted records. If you want to preserve the records, you must move either the records or the extract range.

manipulating your own data using criteria and the Data menu commands. For now, let's get ready for the next section by loading a new copy of INV_LOG.XLT:

1. Save and close INV_LOG2.XLS.

2. Choose INV_LOG.XLT from the bottom of the File menu, and then save the new worksheet that appears with the name INV_LOG3.XLS.

Consolidating Data

An important feature of Excel is the ability to extract totals from sets of data like the sample invoice log, without having to perform multiple sorting operations and multiple SUM functions. Called consolidation, this feature enables Excel to perform several functions on part of the data in a worksheet, based either on a name associated with the data or on its position. Sound confusing? An example will not only clarify the concept of consolidation, but will also give you some ideas about how to make use of it. Let's do a couple of consolidations using INV_LOG3.XLS. First, we'll add the sales amounts by regional office, locating the result of the consolidation at the bottom of the database:

1. Select cell A50 as the top-left corner of the range that Excel will use to report the results of the consolidation.

Setting the consolidate range

2. Choose Consolidate from the Data menu. Excel displays this dialog box:

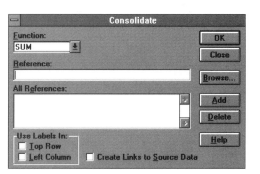

3. The Function drop-down list box contains the functions you can use when consolidating. Leave the default selection, SUM, selected.

4. In the Use Labels In section of the dialog box, select the Left Column option, and check that the Top Row option is not selected. The Left Column option tells Excel to consolidate the information based on the left column of the range referenced in the Reference text box.

5. Click the Reference text box, and type *E5:F48* (the Office and Amount of Sale columns). You could also drag the dialog box out of the way and select the range with the mouse.

6. Click OK. Excel totals the sales amounts for each regional office and puts the results in cells B50:B51, with the East and West labels appearing to the left in A50:A51. (Adjust the column widths as necessary to see the totals.)

Now let's consolidate the amounts by salesperson:

1. Select cell C50 as the top-left corner of the consolidate range.

2. Choose Consolidate from the Data menu.

3. Leave the Function and Use Labels In options just as they are.

4. In the All References list box, select the previous range consolidated, and click the Delete button.

5. Click the Reference text box, type *D5:F48*, and click OK. Excel lists the salespeople's names in column C and their total sales in column E. Excel leaves column D blank, because it can't consolidate the information in the Office column.

Room for consolidation

When you designate a cell as the top-left corner of the consolidate range, be sure there is room below the range for the consolidated information, because Excel overwrites any existing information. Be especially careful if you are unsure how many rows consolidation will require.

Inadvertent consolidation

If you do not delete the range used in the previous consolidation from the All References list box, Excel will consolidate the previous range with any new range you add to the list.

6. Select E50:E56, and move the range to column D using Cell Drag And Drop editing.

Finally, let's total the amounts by quarter:

1. Select cell E50, and choose Consolidate from the Data menu.

2. Leave the Function and Use Labels In options just as they are.

3. In the All References list box, select the previous range consolidated, and then click the Delete button.

4. Click the Reference text box, type B5:F48, and click OK. Excel lists the four quarters in column E and the consolidated amounts in column I, again leaving blank columns for the intervening data.

5. Select I50:I53, and move the totals to column F. Here's the result of the consolidations:

	A	B	C	D	E	F
49						
50	East	$1,775,750.40	Crux, Jamie	$506,849.84	1	$822,216.74
51	West	$1,513,116.56	Olderon, Sam	$363,502.24	2	$822,216.74
52			Karnov, Peter	$836,900.68	3	$822,216.74
53			Smite, Karleena	$169,424.28	4	$822,216.74
54			Crux, Tad	$262,575.60		
55			Furban, Wally	$835,205.80		
56			Ladder, Larry	$314,408.52		
57						

Consolidation by position

In our example, we consolidate by name; that is, we use the category name to consolidate values. If you are working with several worksheets with similar information in the exact same cells, you can consolidate the information by position. Leave the Use Labels In options deselected, and don't select the category labels when adding cell ranges to the All References list box.

Adding consolidation ranges

Using the Add button in the Consolidate dialog box, you can select several different ranges on different worksheets from which you want Excel to consolidate information. Select the ranges, and then click the Add button to add them to the list in the All References list box. Use the Browse button to locate worksheets that aren't open. If you make a mistake, highlight the range in the All References list box, and then click the Delete button. Click OK when you have finished adding ranges. Excel will then consolidate the information from the designated worksheets into the consolidate range on the active worksheet.

Now let's add together the amounts for the salespeople to get a grand total.

1. Select D57.

2. Click the AutoSum tool on the Toolbar, and then click the Enter box. Excel displays the result, $3,288,866.96, in cell D57.

We'll use the consolidated totals later in this chapter, after we have created a couple of worksheets that we can link to INV_LOG3.XLS. To create these worksheets, let's take a detour and learn about another Excel feature—group editing.

Using Groups

Suppose you want to use the information in INV_LOG3.XLS to analyze the performance of your salespeople. You want to create identical worksheets for each person—that's seven worksheets to set up before you can get going with the analysis. In this section, we'll demonstrate how you can use groups of worksheets to reduce that set-up time.

Groups consist of worksheets that you temporarily link together so that any editing or formatting that you do in one is applied to the others. Let's take a closer look. To make it easier for you to follow along, we'll create just two new worksheets, but you can create as many as you need.

Disbanding a group

1. Create two new worksheets by clicking the New Worksheet tool on the toolbar twice.

2. With one of the new worksheets active, click the Save File tool on the toolbar, and then save the file as REV_WFUR.XLS (for *Review: Wally Furban*).

3. Choose the other new worksheet from the Window menu, and save it as REV_PKAR.XLS (for *Review: Peter Karnov*).

4. Choose Group Edit from the Options menu. Excel displays this dialog box:

Excel assumes that you want all open worksheets to be in the group and highlights their names in the dialog box.

5. You want only the new worksheets to be in the group, so deselect INV_LOG3.XLS by holding down the Ctrl key and clicking its name in the list. Then click OK.

Designating group members

6. So that you can see both group worksheets at the same time, choose Arrange from the Window menu.

7. In the Arrange Windows dialog box, select the Documents Of Active Group option, and click OK. Your screen now looks like this:

As you can see, Excel arranges the two group worksheets so that they each take up half the screen. Notice that [Group] appears next to the names in the worksheet title bars to remind you that you are working in a group.

The worksheet that was active when you chose the Group Edit command—REV_PKAR.XLS, in this case—becomes the group "leader." Changes you make to this worksheet are reflected in all other group worksheets. If you activate any other worksheet, Excel disbands the group.

Disbanding a group

Entering and Formatting Text

Let's start by entering a few labels so that the information in these worksheets is easy to understand at a glance:

1. Make the following entries in the active worksheet:

A1	SALES PERFORMANCE, 1992
A3	Name
A4	Base Salary
A5	Commission Rate (%)
A6	Commission
A7	Your Sales
A8	Region's Sales
A9	Total Sales
A10	Sales Expense (%)
A11	Contribution to Region's Sales (%)
A12	Contribution to Total Sales (%)

2. Select A1:A12, and click the Bold tool.

3. Widen column A until all the entries are visible. All the entries and formatting you made in the first worksheet appear in the second, as shown here:

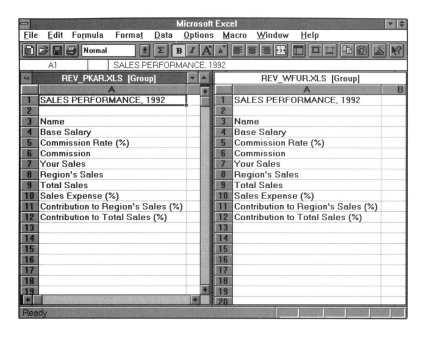

Entering Formulas

Now it's time to get to the heart of the matter. While still in the group, we'll enter some base data and then add the necessary formulas.

1. So that you will have some room to work in, maximize REV_PKAR.XLS by clicking the Maximize button in the window's top-right corner.

2. Make the following entries in the indicated cells, clicking OK when you see the #DIV/0! error message:

B3	Peter Karnov
B4	$18,000
B5	2%
B6	=B5*B7
B10	=(B4+B6)/B7
B11	=B7/B8
B12	=B7/B9

Excel displays #DIV/0! in cells B10:B12 to indicate that the formulas in those cells have a divisor of zero. The error will disappear when you enter values in cells B7:B9.

3. You entered the base salary and the commission rate "in format," as currency and a percentage. As their labels indicate, cells B6:B9 also need to be formatted as currency, so select them, and then select Currency from the Style drop-down list box on the toolbar. Cells B10:B12 need to be

Common error messages

When Excel can't understand what you are attempting to do in a cell, it displays an error value in that cell. The #DIV/0! error is a common error value, indicating that you are attempting to divide by zero. The #N/A error indicates that the formula in the current cell refers to a cell that doesn't contain any information. The #NAME? error value indicates that you have used a name in a formula that Excel can't find in the Define Name dialog box. The #NUM! error value tells you that Excel has found an erroneous argument in a formula requiring a number. The #VALUE! error means that you have created a formula that attempts to perform a mathematical operation with a text value. The #REF! error indicates that you have deleted a cell or range that was included in a formula.

Returning to a group

Excel remembers which worksheets were part of your last group. If you disband the group by selecting another worksheet, you can return to the group by choosing Group Edit from the Options menu and clicking OK.

formatted as percentages, so select them, and then select Percent from the Style drop-down list box.

4. Make column B wider so that you can see the entries.

5. Click the Restore button (the double-headed arrow) at the right end of the menu bar to redisplay the two worksheets side by side.

Saving group worksheets

6. Before we go any further, let's save the worksheets. Choose Save from the File menu. Because the group is still active, all the group worksheets are saved. Here's the result so far:

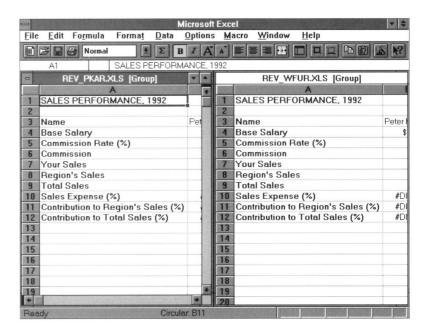

Linking Worksheets

The values you need to enter in cells B6:B8 are available in INV_LOG3.XLS, but, unfortunately, to reference this data you need to make INV_LOG3.XLS the active worksheet, which will dissolve the group. So let's finish these worksheets one by one, linking them to INV_LOG3.XLS as we go.

1. Click anywhere in REV_WFUR.XLS to break up the group. Notice that [Group] disappears from the title bars of both worksheets.

2. Maximize REV_PKAR.XLS, and select cell B7.

3. Type =, choose INV_LOG3.XLS from the Window menu, and click Peter Karnov's sales amount in cell D52. Then click the Enter box. Excel enters the reference to INV_LOG3.XLS in cell B7 and displays the sales amount.

4. Select B8 of REV_PKAR.XLS, type =, choose INV_LOG3.XLS from the Window menu, and click East's sales amount in cell B50. Then click the Enter box.

5. Select B9, type =, choose INV_LOG3.XLS from the Window menu, and click the total sales amount in cell D57. Then click the Enter box. Adjust column B's width. The #DIV/0! errors have been replaced by the formula results, as shown here:

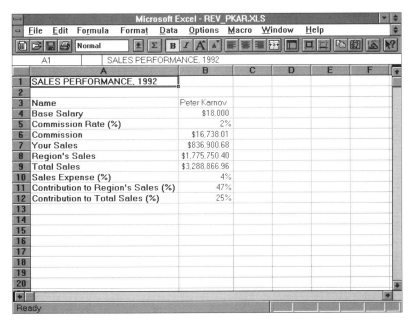

6. Now choose REV_WFUR.XLS from the bottom of the Window menu, change the name in cell B3, and adjust the base salary and commission rate in B4 and B5 to $19,500 and 3% respectively.

7. Repeat steps 3, 4, and 5, clicking cell D55 to enter Wally Furban's sales amount in step 3, clicking B51 to enter West's sales amount in step 4, and then clicking cell D57 to enter the total sales amount in step 5.

You've just learned how to link worksheets. By creating simple formulas in REV_PKAR.XLS and REV_WFUR.XLS that reference cells in INV_LOG3.XLS, you have linked the two performance-review worksheets to the invoice log. Now if the values in the linked cells in INV_LOG3.XLS change, the results of the linking formulas in REV_PKAR.XLS and REV_WFUR.XLS will also change.

External references

The link is carried out by means of an external reference to INV_LOG3.XLS that enables Excel to quickly find the referenced cell and pull information from it. Let's take a look at an external reference.

1. In REV_WFUR.XLS, select cell B9, which contains the total sales amount, and look at the formula bar:

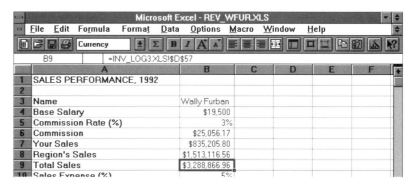

The first part of the reference is the name of the supporting worksheet, INV_LOG3.XLS, followed by an exclamation point. The exclamation point is Excel's clue that the reference is outside the current worksheet. Next comes the absolute

Double duty

Just as double-clicking a cell containing a formula selects all the other cells that the formula uses, double-clicking a cell containing external references simultaneously opens the worksheets that contain the referenced cells and selects the cells themselves.

Q + E

Excel ships with a program called Q+E (for *querying and editing*). You can use this database program to edit and update database files that were created in other database programs.

reference to the cell in INV_LOG3.XLS that contains the total sales amount, $D$57.

2. Hold down the Shift key, and choose Close All from the File menu. Excel prompts you to save each worksheet before it closes them. Click Yes in each case.

Closing all worksheets

We'll leave you to experiment with the linking formulas you have created. Try making and saving a few changes to the amounts in the invoice log, consolidating the amounts, and then closing the log. When you open the performance-review worksheets, Excel asks whether you want to update references to unopened documents. If you click Yes, Excel reads the new values from the unopened INV_LOG3.XLS and updates the performance-review worksheets accordingly.

Updating linked worksheets

Tracking Budgets

4

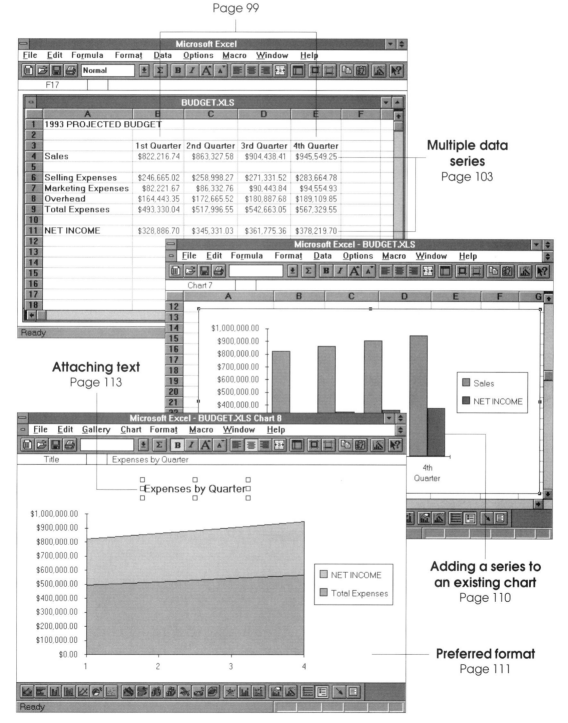

Adjusting multiple column widths
Page 99

Multiple data series
Page 103

Attaching text
Page 113

Adding a series to an existing chart
Page 110

Preferred format
Page 111

In the previous chapters, you learned a lot about Excel, and you now know enough to put Excel to use in your own business environment. After all that hard work, let's relax a bit. Using a budget worksheet as a basis, in this chapter we explore the various ways you can visually present worksheet data.

Setting Up the Budget

We'll start by showing you step by step how to set up this projected budget worksheet:

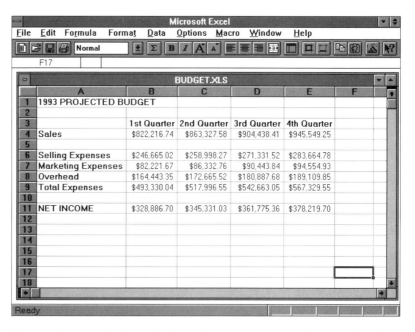

Once the worksheet is in place, we can plot the budget information as various kinds of charts. Assuming that Excel is loaded, follow these steps to create the worksheet:

1. If you do not have a new, blank worksheet on your screen, save and close any open worksheets, and then click the New Worksheet tool on the toolbar.

2. Save the worksheet as BUDGET.XLS.

3. In cell A1, type *1993 PROJECTED BUDGET* as the worksheet title, click the Enter box, and then make the title bold.

4. In cell B3, type *1st Quarter*, and drag the AutoFill pointer to cell E3 (see page 59 for more information about AutoFill). Excel automatically fills the range with the labels 2nd Quarter, 3rd Quarter, and 4th Quarter. Make these labels bold, and center them.

5. Now manually adjust the width of columns B through E so that the labels fit. Instead of selecting one column at a time, select all four columns by clicking the heading of column B and dragging through the heading of column E. Then adjust the width of one of the columns. All four columns take on the new width.

Adjusting multiple
column widths

6. In cell A4, type *Sales*, and click the Enter box. Then make the Sales label bold.

7. Next, enter these sales amounts in the indicated cells:

B4	$822,216.74
C4	$863,327.58
D4	$904,438.41
E4	$945,549.25

Now let's tackle the expenses. For this example, assume that we have selling expenses that average 30 percent of sales, marketing expenses that average 10 percent, and overhead expenses (fixed costs) that average 20 percent.

1. Enter the following information in the indicated cells:

A6	Selling Expenses
A7	Marketing Expenses
A8	Overhead
A9	Total Expenses
B6	=.3*B4
B7	=.1*B4
B8	=.2*B4
B9	=SUM(B6:B8)

2. Select B6:B9, and drag the AutoFill pointer to column E to duplicate the 1st quarter formulas for the 2nd, 3rd, and 4th quarters.

3. Select B4:E11, and then select Currency from the Style drop-down list box on the toolbar.

4. Select A6:A11, and click the Bold tool on the toolbar. Then choose Column Width from the Format menu, and click the Best Fit button.

Finally, let's compute the net income:

1. In cell A11, type *NET INCOME*, and press Tab to enter the label and select B11.

2. With B11 selected, type an equal sign, select B4, type a minus sign (–), select B9, and then click the Enter box. Excel enters the result, $328,886.70, as the 1st quarter's net income.

3. Use AutoFill to copy the formula in cell B11 to cells C11:E11.

Viola! Your budget worksheet should now look like the one shown earlier.

Creating Charts in the Worksheet Environment

With Excel, you can create charts in two ways: as separate documents or on the worksheet. In this section, we show you how to quickly plot data on the worksheet. The advantage of this method is that you can then save and print the chart and the underlying worksheet as one document. We'll create the

Outlining worksheets

Excel's outlining feature lets you view as little or as much of a worksheet as you want to see. It searches for what it considers to be the most important information (for example, totals) and uses this information to create different row and column outline levels. When you are in outline mode, you can click a button to view different levels of your worksheet.

To outline a range, select the range, and choose Outline from the Formula menu. Accept the default settings, and click the Create button.

Initially, an outlined worksheet displays all its levels. You use up to seven row level buttons to expand and collapse the outline. For example, clicking the 2 button displays only the first and second levels and hides any lower levels.

You can also click buttons labeled with minus signs to collapse an outline level. Excel deduces that the last row of a section is the "bottom line" of the collapsed section and displays only that row. Conversely, you can click buttons labeled with plus signs to expand collapsed levels.

chart using a new Excel 4 feature: the ChartWizard. In previous versions of Excel, we would first create the chart and then open it in the chart environment to format it. ChartWizard automates the otherwise complex process of creating and then formatting charts.

To create worksheet charts, you use the ChartWizard tool on the Standard toolbar:

1. Select A3:E4, and click the ChartWizard tool.

2. Move the cross-hair pointer to the blank area below your worksheet entries, hold down the mouse button, and drag to create a marquee about the size of the worksheet window. Then release the mouse button.

Drawing the chart frame

3. ChartWizard displays the first of five dialog boxes to lead you through the process of creating and customizing a chart. These dialog boxes are labeled by step—Step 1 of 5, Step 2 of 5, and so on. In the first dialog box, click Next to confirm that you want the range you selected to be charted and move to the next dialog box.

4. In the second dialog box, select 3-D Column as the chart format, and then click Next.

5. In the third dialog box, accept the default 3-D column type, and click Next.

6. In the fourth dialog box, Excel displays how the selected range will look as a chart, with all labels and other information in place. At this point, or any other point in the chart-creating process, you can click the Back button to move one step back in the process and select a different format. In this case, accept the default settings, and move to the next dialog box by clicking Next.

Changing chart formats

7. In the final dialog box, click No as the Add A Legend option. Excel updates the Sample Chart area of the dialog box to reflect this change.

8. Click OK. Excel displays the chart shown on the next page.

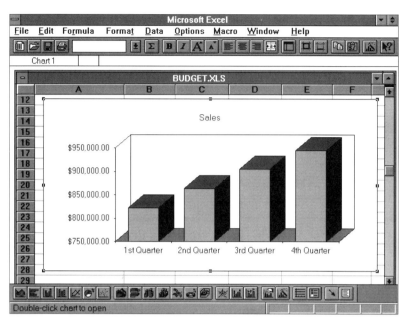

Excel has drawn a 3-D column chart of the data in A3:E4, with the 1st, 2nd, 3rd, and 4th Quarter labels along the x-axis (the horizontal axis) and dollar amounts at regular intervals along the y-axis (the vertical axis). The label from cell A4, Sales, has been used as the chart's title.

Displaying the Chart toolbar

Excel also displays the Chart toolbar at the bottom of the screen. (If you don't see the Chart toolbar, display it by using the toolbar shortcut menu.)

Chart labels

If you include column or row labels when selecting the data you want Excel to chart, Excel uses them as axis labels, whether you are creating a worksheet chart or an independent chart document.

Moving and sizing

You can move a worksheet chart anywhere on the screen by dragging it. You can make it larger or smaller by dragging one of the black squares, or handles, around its frame in the direction in which you want the frame to grow.

Preferred format

By default, Excel creates worksheet charts in what's called the Preferred format. When you first start Excel, the Preferred format is a plain column chart. See page 111 for information about how to change the Preferred format.

We have plotted only one set of data, called a data series. Let's see what the chart looks like when we plot two series:

1. The single-series worksheet chart should be active. (Black squares, called handles, appear around the chart's perimeter to indicate that it is active.) If it isn't, simply click it.

Deleting worksheet charts

2. Press the Del key to delete the chart.

3. Select A3:E4 again. Then select a second series by holding down the Ctrl key and selecting A11:E11.

Multiple data series

4. Click the ChartWizard tool, and drag another marquee in the blank area below the worksheet entries.

5. In the first dialog box, accept all the ChartWizard default options in all the dialog boxes by clicking the >> button. Excel displays the selected data in its default two-dimensional column chart format, with a legend:

Adding a legend

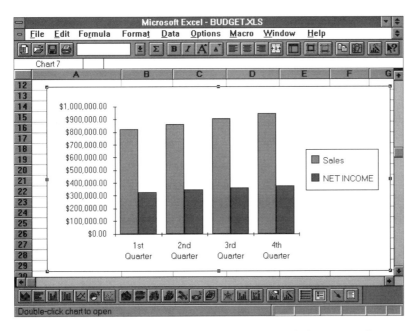

The new chart has no title because Excel does not know which of the two labels, Sales or NET INCOME, to use. The sales amounts and net-income amounts are grouped in quarters and are represented by columns of different colors or shades. The legend identifies each of the two series by matching color or shade.

Automatic updating

Worksheet charts are actively linked to the data Excel uses to plot them, and they automatically change if the data changes. Try this:

1. Change one of the net-income figures. The net-income column grows or shrinks to reflect the change.

2. Choose Undo Entry from the Edit menu to undo the change.

Formatting Worksheet Charts

As you have just seen, creating worksheet charts is very easy. You simply select the data, click the ChartWizard tool, and create the chart frame. Excel fills in all the details. If you want to format this chart or change it to a different type (see page 107 for more about chart types), you need to open the chart in the chart environment, or use the Chart toolbar. We'll show you how to use the Chart toolbar first.

Using the first three groups of buttons on the Chart toolbar, you can instantly change the chart type. Let's try a few of these buttons now:

1. Check that the worksheet chart is selected.

Creating 3-D pie charts

2. Experiment by clicking different chart tools. For example, if you click the 3-D Pie Chart tool, Excel formats the chart to look like this:

Chart scale

If you change the source data radically, the scale of the entire chart might change. For example, if you enter a sales amount in the millions in BUDGET.XLS, the other columns shrink down to almost nothing to keep the scale consistent.

Source format

If you change the format of the source data—for example, if you select B4:E11 in BUDGET.XLS, choose Number from the Format menu, and then select a Currency format with no decimal places ($#,##0)—the labels along the y-axis change accordingly.

Underlying values

The format of the values in your worksheet does not affect the way they are plotted. Excel always uses the underlying values when plotting charts.

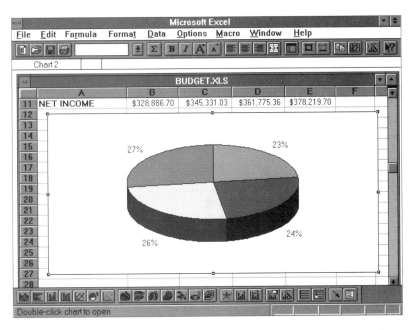

As you try different chart types, notice that the selected data doesn't format well (or at all) in some types. For example, the 3-D pie format displays only one data series. Excel doesn't discard the information it can't format, however, as you'll see if you try another chart type.

3. Click the 3-D Column Chart tool, and then click the Horizontal Gridlines tool (the fourth button from the right on the Chart toolbar). Excels displays a chart like this one:

Creating 3-D column charts with gridlines

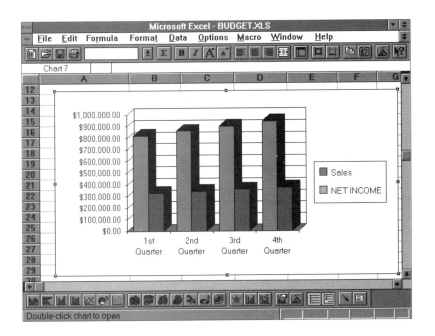

To make any changes to the chart other than the rudimentary changes allowed by the Chart toolbar, you have to open the chart in the chart environment. Try this:

**Opening charts
in the chart environment**

1. Double-click anywhere inside the chart frame. The chart now appears inside a window in the chart environment with the name of the worksheet followed by the word *Chart* and a number in its title bar:

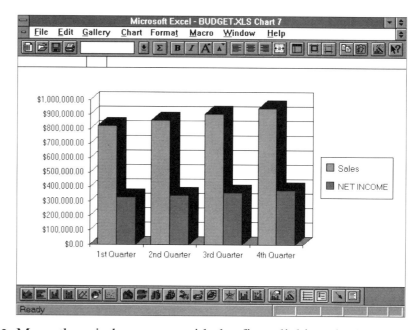

2. Move the window to one side by first clicking the Restore button at the right end of the menu bar and then dragging the chart's title bar. As you can see, the original worksheet chart still resides on the worksheet. You are, in effect, working with a copy of the chart.

3. Click the Maximize button in the window's top-right corner. Excel enlarges the chart window to fill the entire screen.

4. Save this chart by choosing Save As from the File menu, typing *budget1*, and clicking OK. Excel automatically identifies the file as a chart document by adding the extension XLC to the filename.

Now let's take a look at the chart environment. The menu bar no longer has a Formula, Data, or Options menu, but it has gained a Gallery and a Chart menu. If you pull down the

Big charts

A chart in an independent chart document can be only as large as the screen. However, you can make a chart in a worksheet very large because you can scroll the chart frame beyond the edge of the screen. Practical uses of this undocumented feature might be limited, but it's fun to play with!

Format menu, you'll see that its commands have changed significantly so that you can format charts to look their best.

No matter what kind of chart you need—column, bar, pie, line, and so on—Excel has a format that will do the job. Usually, you can come up with impressive visual support for your worksheets by carefully selecting from among Excel's many predefined chart types. We take a look at these next.

Changing the Chart Type

Excel organizes its built-in chart types into galleries that you can access from the Gallery menu. The available chart types include:

Predefined charts

- Column charts (the default type, or preferred format), which are ideal for showing the variations in the value of an item over time, as with the budget example.

- Bar charts, which are great for showing the values of several items at a single point in time. (The "columns" representing the values are rotated 90 degrees so that they are horizontal.)

- Line charts, which are often used to show variations in the value of more than one item over time.

- Area charts, which look something like line charts but which plot multiple data series as cumulative layers with different colors, patterns, or shades.

The SERIES function

If you click one of the columns in the chart document, a SERIES function appears in the formula bar. This function links the chart to the source worksheet. Notice that the external references are all absolute. If you change the position of the charted data in the source worksheet, Excel will not be able to find the moved data.

Updating linked data

Each time you open a chart document without opening the linked worksheet that contains the chart data, Excel displays the message *Update references to unopened documents?* When you click the Yes button, Excel looks at the unopened worksheet to see if the data has changed, and if it has, Excel changes the chart accordingly.

- Pie charts, which are ideal for showing the percentages of an item that can be assigned to the item's components. (Pie charts can plot only one data series.)

- XY (or scatter) charts, which are used to detect correlations between independent items (such as a person's height and weight).

- Radar charts, which plot each series on its own axes radiating from a center point.

- 3-D charts, which add a third dimension to column, line, area, and pie charts. One type of 3-D chart not available in a two-dimensional format is the 3-D Surface chart.

In addition, you can create various kinds of combination charts, which plot one type of chart on top of another as an "overlay."

Each gallery offers several variations that will satisfy most of your charting needs. Let's try changing the type of the chart currently on your screen so that you can see some of the possibilities:

Creating bar charts

1. Choose Bar from the Gallery menu, select format 6, and then click OK.

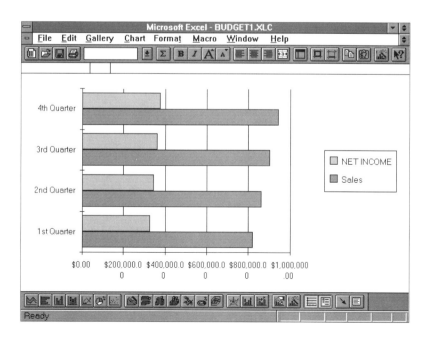

2. Next, choose Line from the Gallery menu, select format 1, and click OK.

Creating line charts

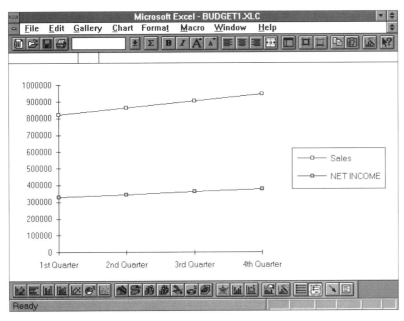

3. Return to the previous version of the chart by choosing 3-D Column from the Gallery menu. Then select format 4, and click OK.

4. Choose the Close command from the File menu, click Yes to save the chart and return it to the worksheet, and then save BUDGET.XLS.

Rotating 3-D charts

You can use the 3-D View command on the Format menu to adjust the angle of a 3-D chart, but there is an easier way. In the chart environment, click one of the corners of the chart, and drag the handle that appears. Excel displays a wire "skeleton" of the chart, which you can rotate to the desired angle. Then, when you release the mouse button, Excel redraws the chart.

Because you must use one of the corner handles, 3-D pie charts can be rotated only with the 3-D View command.

Chart conversion

After creating a chart in the chart environment, you can easily paste it into an Excel worksheet as a worksheet chart. First choose Select Chart from the Chart menu, and then choose Copy from the Edit menu. Select the worksheet, and choose Paste from the Edit menu. The chart appears in the worksheet, where you can move or size it as needed.

You might want to spend some time becoming familiar with the other predefined formats so that you have an idea of what's available.

Creating Charts in the Chart Environment

The traditional method of creating a chart in Excel is to plot the data directly in the chart environment and then format the chart there. The chart and its source data are linked, and Excel updates the chart to reflect any changes made to the data. Let's experiment, again using the budget worksheet:

Creating new charts

1. Select A3:E4, and choose New from the File menu. Excel displays the New dialog box.

2. Select Chart, and click OK to create a new chart document. Excel uses the data in the selected range to plot a simple column chart:

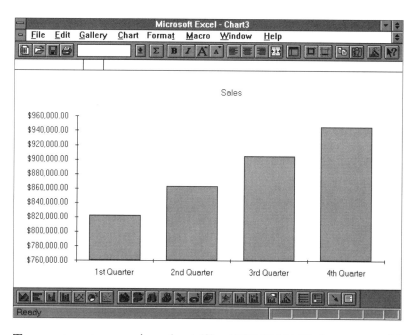

To create a two-series chart like BUDGET1.XLC, you could start all over, but there is an easier way:

Adding a series to an existing chart

1. Make the BUDGET.XLS worksheet active, select A11:E11, and then choose Copy from the Edit menu.

2. Make the new chart active, and choose Paste from the Edit menu. Excel pastes in the second data series. Using this technique, you can create charts piecemeal from many different sources.

Changing the Preferred Format

When you first create a chart in the traditional way, Excel uses the Preferred format, which by default is a plain column chart. If the data you work with most often is better presented in a different format, you can change the Preferred format so that Excel always uses that chart type instead. Here's how to make an area chart the Preferred format:

1. Choose Area from the Gallery menu, select format 1, and click OK. The chart now looks similar to the line chart you saw earlier, except that the area below each line is filled in.

Creating area charts

2. With the area chart on your screen, choose Set Preferred from the Gallery menu.

3. Close the chart without saving it.

Excel has changed the Preferred format both for charts you create on the worksheet and charts you create in the chart environment. Follow these steps to be sure that the change has been made:

1. In BUDGET.XLS, hold down the Ctrl key, select the ranges A9:E9 and A11:E11 in the worksheet, and then click the

Combining for contrast

When you want to contrast two or more series or emphasize a significant relationship, try plotting your data as a combination chart. Combination charts consist of a main chart of one type and an overlay chart of another type. A common combination is a main column chart and a line overlay chart.

Adjusting chart data

When your data doesn't need to be exact, you can "fudge" a little to make a column, bar, line, or scatter chart look better. Hold down Ctrl, and click to select the column, bar, or data point you want to change. When a black dot appears, drag it to the desired position. The source data in the worksheet changes accordingly. Note that this technique works only with two-dimensional charts.

ChartWizard tool. Next, define a new chart area below the current one, and click the >> button. Excel plots the two data series—Total Expenses and NET INCOME—in the new Preferred format, as shown here:

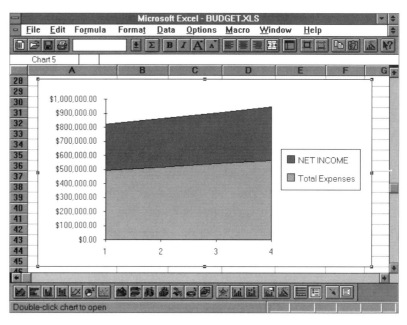

2. Double-click the chart to open it in the chart environment, and then save it as a chart document using the name Excel suggests.

Formatting in the Chart Environment

When a chart is open in the chart environment, you can add and format chart elements using commands on the Chart and Format menus. One menu command worth looking at more closely is the Add Text command, found on the Chart menu. You can also spellcheck a chart using the Spelling command, just as you can spellcheck a worksheet or macro sheet. As with the Gallery menu, many of the choices on the Chart and Format menus duplicate actions performed by tools on the Chart toolbar. Use whichever method is easiest for you.

Shortcut menus

Shortcut menus exist for almost every conceivable chart element. Experiment by clicking chart elements (gridlines, axes, series, and so on) with the right mouse button to open their shortcut menus. When you've finished experimenting on your own, we'll show you how to add a title to the chart now on your screen.

Adding a Title

Because you selected more than one data series when you created the chart on your screen, Excel was unable to determine what the chart's title should be. Here's how you add a title to a multi-series chart:

1. Choose Attach Text from the Chart menu or the chart's shortcut menu. Excel displays this dialog box:

Attaching text

As you can see, you can also use the options in the Attach Text dialog box to add labels to many elements of the chart.

2. Accept the default selection, Chart Title, by clicking OK. Excel adds the word *Title* to the top of the chart.

3. In the formula bar, replace *Title* with *Expenses by Quarter*, and click the Enter box. The result is shown on the next page.

Chart toolbars oddities

Using the Arrow and the Text Box tools produces different results depending on whether you are working on a worksheet chart or on a chart in the chart environment. If you add an arrow or a text box to a worksheet chart using these tools, they disappear when you open the chart in the chart environment. You can then use the tools (or the equivalent commands on the Chart menu) to add the arrow or text box again. But when you go back to the worksheet, the missing items return, and you then have two arrows or two text boxes!

Legend labels

If you don't include labels when you select data to be plotted, Excel assigns the labels Series1, Series2, and so on to the keys in the legend. To change these labels, choose Edit Series from the Chart menu. In the Edit Series dialog box, select Series1 in the Series list box, and type the new name in the Name text box. Then click the Define button. Repeat this process for each label, and then click OK.

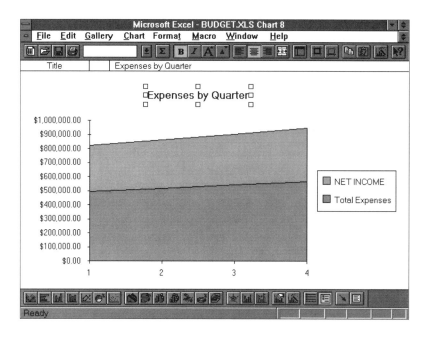

Creating Picture Charts

Graphics in charts

Before we discuss printing charts, we can't resist mentioning an Excel feature that allows you to use graphics created in programs such as Paintbrush to plot data series in column or bar charts. You start by creating a two-dimensional column or bar chart in Excel. Then you create a simple graphic element in a Windows graphics program and copy it. After activating the Excel chart, you select the series you want the graphic to replace and choose Paste. Excel then substitutes the graphic for the data-series marker, distorting it to fill the area formerly occupied by the column or bar. You can then fill the area with repeating graphics instead, by choosing the Patterns command from the Format menu and selecting one of the Stack options. Here's an example of a picture chart:

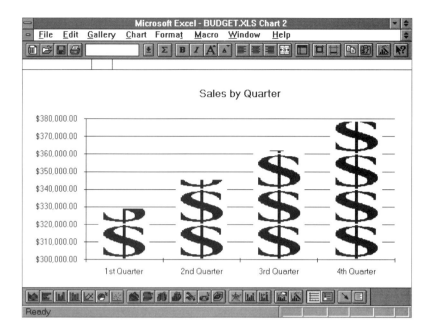

Printing Charts

Printing charts is much like printing worksheets. The main
difference concerns the Page Setup dialog box, which allows
you to specify whether the chart should be printed the same
size as it appears on the screen (Size On Screen), enlarged
proportionally until it fits within the specified page margins
(Scale To Fit Page), or enlarged to fit without regard to
width:height ratios (Use Full Page). You can preview a chart,
but because a chart document can never be more than one
page, the Next and Previous buttons are not available. Otherwise, the basic procedure is the same, and you should have
no difficulty obtaining paper copies of your charts.

**Size options
for printing charts**

5

Estimating Project Costs

Employee-
information table
Page 119

Pasting an
external reference
Page 122

Overhead
table
Page 120

Estimate
worksheet
Page 124

The Iteration option
Page 130

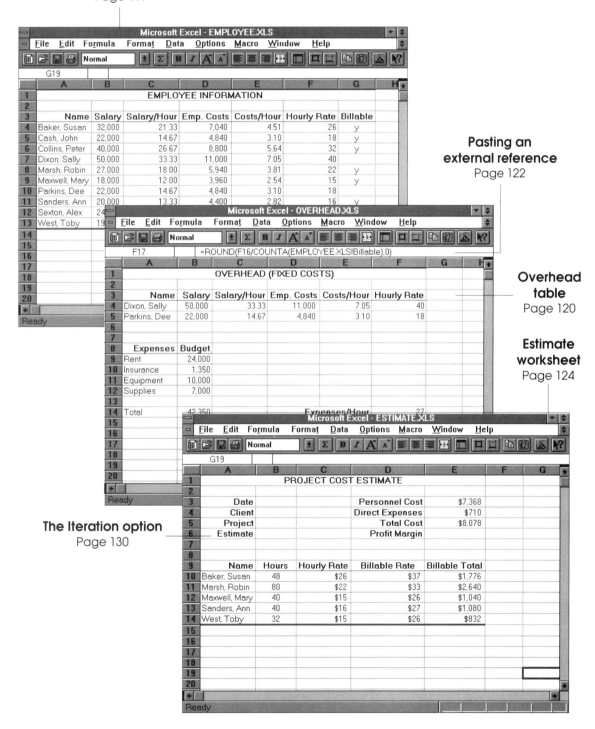

In this chapter, we tackle a more ambitious set of work-sheets. First we create tables of employee information and overhead costs. Then we create a worksheet that estimates project costs by "looking up" hourly rates in one of the tables. Finally, we cover a technique called *iteration*, which enables Excel to resolve circular calculations.

Worksheet ideas

In our example, we create only employee-information and overhead tables because the primary cost involved in the sample project estimate is for people's time. However, you can easily adapt the project cost estimate worksheet to also use a marketing-expenses or materials-information table. For example, if you manage a construction business that specializes in bathroom and kitchen remodeling, you can create a table with up-to-date prices for fixtures, plumbing supplies, cabinets, tile, and so on, in addition to the employee-information and overhead tables. If you are a one-person operation and have no employees, you can still adapt the worksheet to make sure that you include overhead and marketing costs in your project estimates.

This chapter differs from previous chapters in that we don't bog down the instructions with information you already know. For example, we might show you a worksheet and ask you to create it, without telling you step by step what to enter, how to make an entry bold, and how to adjust column widths. We leave it up to you to create the worksheet using the illustration as a guide. Similarly, we might tell you to create a formula, assuming that you know how to paste functions into cells (to review the procedure, turn to page 54) and how to use cell references as arguments (see page 40).

Creating the Supporting Tables

The logical way to begin this example is to enter the data needed for the two supporting tables. There's nothing complicated about these tables; we've stripped them down so that you don't have to type any extraneous information. The few calculations involved have been greatly simplified and do not reflect the gyrations accountants would go through to ensure to-the-penny accuracy. So instead of describing how to create these tables, we'll simply show them to you and, after discussing the few formulas and cell and range names involved, let you create them on your own.

1. In a blank worksheet, create the table of employee information shown below, and then save it as EMPLOYEE.XLS. Row 4 of this worksheet uses these formulas:

Employee-information table

C4	=B4/50/30 *Annual salary divided by 50 weeks (allowing 2 weeks for vacation), divided by 30 billable hours per week (allowing 2 hours per day of non-billable time)*
D4	=B4*22% *Employer contributions to social security and benefits estimated at 22 percent of annual salary*
E4	=D4/52/30 *Employer contributions to social security and benefits divided by 52 weeks divided by 30 hours per week*
F4	=ROUND(C4+E4,0) *Salary per hour plus benefits per hour, rounded to a whole number (0 decimal places)*

The ROUND function

Microsoft Excel - EMPLOYEE.XLS

File Edit Formula Format Data Options Macro Window Help

G19

	A	B	C	D	E	F	G	H
1			EMPLOYEE INFORMATION					
2								
3	Name	Salary	Salary/Hour	Emp. Costs	Costs/Hour	Hourly Rate	Billable	
4	Baker, Susan	32,000	21.33	7,040	4.51	26	y	
5	Cash, John	22,000	14.67	4,840	3.10	18	y	
6	Collins, Peter	40,000	26.67	8,800	5.64	32	y	
7	Dixon, Sally	50,000	33.33	11,000	7.05	40		
8	Marsh, Robin	27,000	18.00	5,940	3.81	22	y	
9	Maxwell, Mary	18,000	12.00	3,960	2.54	15	y	
10	Parkins, Dee	22,000	14.67	4,840	3.10	18		
11	Sanders, Ann	20,000	13.33	4,400	2.82	16	y	
12	Sexton, Alex	24,000	16.00	5,280	3.38	19	y	
13	West, Toby	19,000	12.67	4,180	2.68	15	y	
14								
15								
16								
17								
18								
19								
20								

Ready

2. After entering these formulas in row 4, use the Fill Down or AutoFill command to copy them to rows 5 through 13. Then use the AutoFormat tool to make the table more readable.

3. Use Define Name to assign the name Billable to cells G4:G14 and the name Emp_Rate to cells A4:F14. (See page 41 for information about how to assign range names.) We'll use these names in future formulas.

Overhead table → 4. Open a new worksheet, create this overhead table, and save the worksheet as OVERHEAD.XLS:

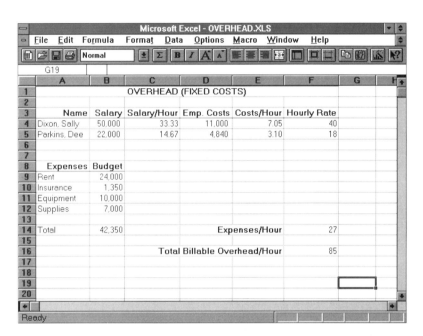

Ascending order

You can list employees in the employee-information table in any order, but before Excel can use the table to look up information, you must sort it in ascending order. Excel cannot look up information in randomly ordered tables or in tables in descending order. Select the range, and choose the Sort command from the Data menu to sort the table.

Extending range names

It is a good idea to always include a blank row or column at the end of the range when assigning range names. If you need to add employees to the EMPLOYEE.XLS worksheet, for example, you can select the blank row below the last entry and choose the Insert command from the Edit menu to extend the range with the name Billable.

Flexible formulas

Keep in mind that using names in formulas makes your worksheets much more flexible than if you use cell references. If the information referenced in a formula moves because of changes you make to a worksheet, Excel adjusts the definition of the name so that it continues to access the correct information.

Sally Dixon and Dee Parkins are administrative employees who do not directly generate income for the company, so we need to include their salaries and benefits in this overhead calculation. You can copy their entries from the EMPLOYEE.XLS worksheet or enter them from scratch. Again, here are the formulas to use in row 4:

C4	=B4/50/30
D4	=B4*22%
E4	=D4/52/30
F4	=ROUND(C4+E4,0)

5. If you are entering the formulas from scratch, use Fill Down or AutoFill to copy the entries in row 4 to row 5.

6. Next, enter these formulas in the designated cells:

B14	=SUM(B9:B12)
F14	=ROUND(B14/52/30,0)
F16	=SUM(F4:F14)

We must bill 30 hours each week at the rate in F16 to cover overhead costs. We cannot bill overhead to a client directly, so we must increase the hourly rate of employees with billable hours by a prorated amount to ensure that overhead is included in project estimates. To calculate the prorated overhead amount, we need to divide the total billable rate per hour in cell F16 by the number of employees who generate income. We can glance at the employee-information worksheet and

Cell notes

To annotate a cell to explain its contents, select the cell, and choose Note from the Formula menu. In the Text Note section of the Cell Note dialog box, type a sentence or two explaining the cell, and then click OK. Excel displays a small square in the top-right corner of the cell to indicate that a note is attached. Double-click the cell to display the note.

Users with sound recording equipment attached to their computer can create sound notes. Use the Record, Play, and Import buttons in the Sound Note section of the Cell Note dialog box to create the note. To play back the note, you must have a sound board or MIDI equipment. Simply double-click the cell to play back the sound.

know that this number is eight, but what if the company had many employees? We would want Excel to supply this number for us. Here's how.

Counting Entries

The COUNTA function

We can tell Excel to count the number of employees that have a Y in the Billable column of EMPLOYEE.XLS by using the COUNTA function. This function has only one argument, which is the range of cells we want Excel to scan for entries. Here's how to use COUNTA in the formula that calculates the overhead allocation:

1. In cell E17 of OVERHEAD.XLS, type *Prorated Overhead/Hour*, click the Enter box, and click the Bold and Right Align tools.

2. We want the prorated amount to be in whole dollars, so we need to nest the prorated calculation in a ROUND function. In cell F17, type the following:

   =ROUND(F16/COUNTA(

Pasting an external reference

To divide the hourly overhead in cell F16 by the number of employees whose hours are billable, first choose the EMPLOYEE.XLS worksheet from the Window menu, and then choose the Paste Name command from the Formula menu. Excel displays this dialog box:

COUNTA vs. COUNT

Don't confuse the COUNTA function with the COUNT function. COUNTA tells you how many cells in the selected range contain entries, whereas COUNT tells you how many cells in the range contain numeric values.

Easy opening of linked worksheets

Although Excel will update external references without opening the referenced worksheets, you can easily open all supporting worksheets by choosing the Links command from the File menu. Excel displays a dialog box listing all documents that are referred to by formulas in the active worksheet. Simply select the files you want to open, and click the Open button.

Select Billable, and click OK. Excel follows the opening parenthesis in the formula bar with an external reference to the range named Billable in the EMPLOYEE.XLS worksheet, thereby linking the two worksheets. Next, type a) to close the COUNTA function. Then type a comma, a zero, and a final) to close the ROUND function.

3. Check that the following function is in the formula bar:

=ROUND(F16/COUNTA(EMPLOYEE.XLS!Billable),0)

and then click the Enter box. Excel calculates the formula and enters the value 11 in cell F17.

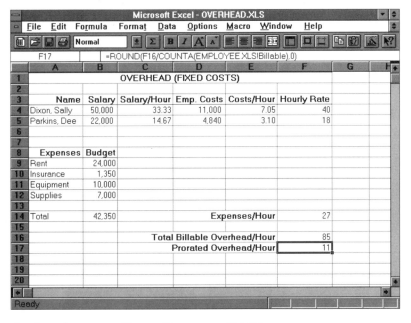

The Spelling command

Use the Spelling command on the Options menu to check the spelling in your worksheets, macro sheets, and charts. Try to check spelling before you add proper nouns to your documents, because Excel's dictionary will probably not recognize them.

4. Assign the name Over_Rate to cell F17.

Creating the Estimate Worksheet

With the two tables in place, we're ready to create the work-sheet for estimating project costs. We'll put the basic structure of the worksheet together first, and then we'll fill in the for-mulas necessary for the calculations.

1. Begin by creating the worksheet shown below, and saving it as ESTIMATE.XLS. The hours next to the employee names are the number of hours you anticipate each will need to work on this project.

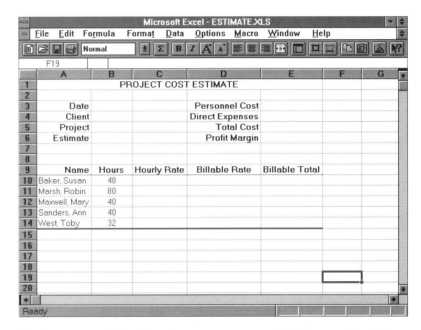

So far, everything has been pretty straightforward and has provided you with nothing more challenging than an oppor-tunity to practice skills you learned in other chapters. Now we need to introduce the Excel function that will enable us to use one of the tables we created earlier to fill in the informa-tion needed for this worksheet.

Looking Up Information

Excel has three functions you can use in formulas to look up information in worksheet tables: LOOKUP (a generic function), VLOOKUP (which is for vertically oriented tables), and HLOOKUP (which is for horizontally oriented tables). Here, we'll show you how to use LOOKUP.

Excel needs two pieces of information to carry out the LOOKUP function: the value you want it to look up and the location of the lookup table. You supply these two pieces of information in this way:

<------   **The LOOKUP function**

=LOOKUP(*value to look for,range to look in*)

If the lookup table has more rows than columns, Excel assumes that it is to search the leftmost column of the table for the value you supply and then enter in the worksheet the value that is in the rightmost column of the table in the same row. For example, to look up the hourly rate for John Cash in the employee-information table, you can enter this function, say in cell A19 of EMPLOYEE.XLS:

=LOOKUP("Cash, John",A4:F13)

Because the employee-information table has more rows than columns, Excel scans the leftmost column—column A—for the text value Cash, John. When it finds the value it's looking for in cell A5, it looks along row 5 to the rightmost column and displays in cell A19 the value 18 from cell F5.

If the employee-information table had more columns than rows, Excel would look for the value you supply in the top row of the table and would enter in the formula cell the value that is in the bottom row of the same column.

Let's see how to put the LOOKUP function to work in the project cost estimate worksheet:

1. Select cell C10 of ESTIMATE.XLS, and choose Paste Function from the Formula menu.

Controlling LOOKUP

If the employee-information table had more columns than rows, we would need to use the VLOOKUP function instead of the LOOKUP function in order to force Excel to search the leftmost column for the supplied value instead of the topmost row.

2. Type L to scroll quickly to functions that begin with the letter L, and scroll down to the LOOKUP function. Select LOOKUP, check that the Paste Arguments option is selected, and click OK. Click OK in the next dialog box that appears. Excel enters the function in the formula bar with the first argument highlighted.

3. Click cell A10, which contains the name of the first employee whose hourly rate we want to look up. The cell reference replaces the first argument in the LOOKUP function in the formula bar.

4. Highlight the LOOKUP function's second argument.

5. Choose EMPLOYEE.XLS from the Window menu, and then choose Paste Name from the Formula menu. In the Paste Name dialog box, select Emp_Rate, and click OK. Excel replaces the LOOKUP function's second argument with an external reference to the name assigned to the lookup table in EMPLOYEE.XLS.

6. Click the Enter box. Excel then looks up the value in cell A10 (Barker, Susan) in the table called Emp_Rate in the EMPLOYEE.XLS worksheet and enters the corresponding hourly rate, as shown here:

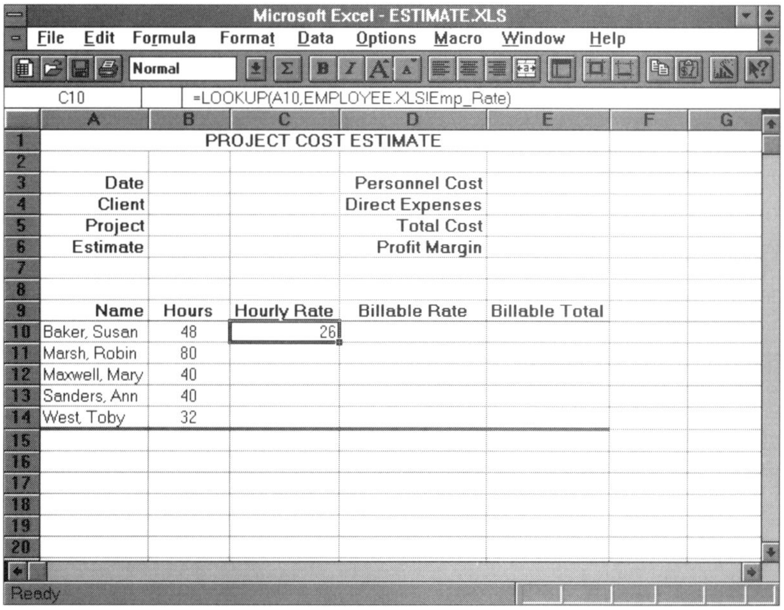

7. Now all you have to do is use Fill Down or AutoFill to copy the formula in C10 to cells C11:C14. Then equivalent formulas will look up the hourly rates for the other people who will be involved in this project.

Completing the Estimate

Well, the hard part is over. A few simple calculations, and you'll be ready to prepare an estimate for your client.

1. In ESTIMATE.XLS, enter these formulas in the indicated cells:

D10	=C10+OVERHEAD.XLS!Over_Rate
E10	=B10*D10

2. Use Fill Down or AutoFill to copy the formulas to D11:E14, like this:

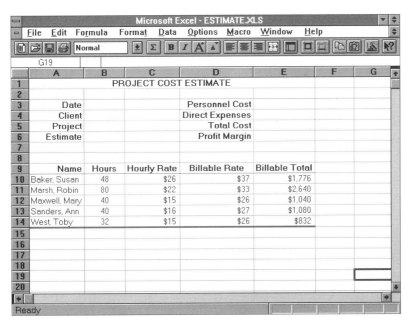

Now you can calculate total costs in the summary area at the top of the worksheet:

1. Make these entries in the indicated cells:

E3	=SUM(E10:E14)
E4	710
E5	=E3+E4

The entry in cell E4 is an estimate of charges that will be incurred for long-distance phone calls, delivery services, and other expenses attributable directly to this project.

2. Select the Currency [0] style from the Style drop-down list to format the cells in the ranges E3:E6 and C10:E14. Then fix the bottom border of the table, which was overwritten when you used Fill Down or AutoFill.

As you can see, the worksheet is almost complete:

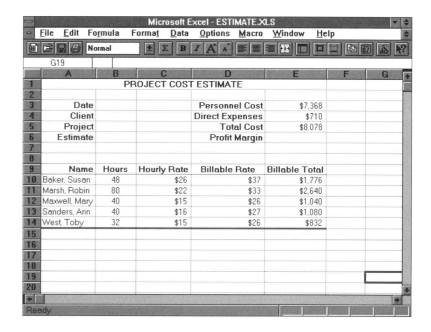

Projecting Profit Margin with Iteration

Probably the most difficult part of estimating a project is figuring out the profit margin. We now have a good idea what this project is going to cost. But suppose we need a margin of roughly 35 percent of the estimate total to be sure we make a profit. How do we calculate the actual profit margin when we don't yet know the estimate total, and how do we calculate the estimate total when we don't know the profit margin? We could go in circles forever.

Fortunately, we can have Excel go in circles for us. Using the iteration technique, we can force Excel to calculate the margin formula over and over until it can give us an answer. Follow these steps:

1. Select cell E6, and enter this formula:

=35%*B6

2. Select cell B6, and enter this formula:

=SUM(E5:E6)

When you enter the second formula, Excel displays this message box:

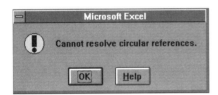

After you click OK, the message *Circular:E6* appears in the status bar, telling you that the formula in E6 is the culprit. This formula multiplies the sum of cells E5 and E6 (the formula in cell B6) by 35 percent. Excel cannot arrive at a result because when it adds E5 and E6, the formula in E6 must be recalculated; and when Excel recalculates the formula, E6 changes, so E5 and E6 must be added again; and so on, forever.

Circular references

Here's how to force Excel to come up with an answer:

1. Choose Calculation from the Options menu. Excel displays the dialog box shown on the next page.

Zero result

When a worksheet contains a circular reference, Excel usually displays 0 as the result of the formula, even if you make adjustments to the values.

Worksheet recalculation

Every time you save and open a worksheet, Excel recalculates it. When Excel recalculates a worksheet that contains a circular reference, the program always displays the *Cannot resolve circular references* message.

Manual calculation

The Manual Calculation option tells Excel to calculate open worksheets only when you click the Calc Now button in the Calculation Options dialog box or press F9. You can activate this option for large worksheets, where recalculating each formula can take some time. The Recalculate Before Save option is selected by default when you turn on Manual Calculation.

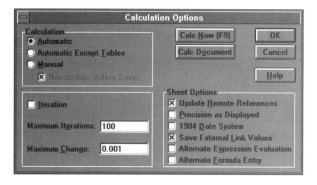

The Iteration option

2. Select the Iteration option, and click OK. You return to the worksheet, where Excel quickly recalculates the formulas, finally coming up with these results:

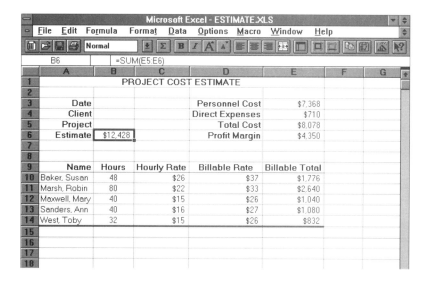

Date calculation

Excel calculates values for dates as the number of days that have elapsed between January 1, 1900 and the date you specify. If you enter 2-Jan-1900 in a cell, the date has a value of 2, meaning that it is the second day following the base date. If you plan to transfer worksheets containing dates to Excel for the Macintosh, you must choose the Calculation Options dialog box's 1904 Date System option. Selecting this option recalculates dates on a base date of January 2, 1904.

Precision of values

The Precision As Displayed option tells Excel to use the value displayed in the cell in formulas rather than the underlying value. For example, if a formula refers to a cell that holds the value 15.386, but displays 15.4 because of column width, this option tells Excel to use 15.4 in the formula.

By selecting the Iteration option, you tell Excel to ignore the circular reference and to keep recalculating the formula, going in circles until it comes up with the best possible results. By default, Excel recalculates the formulas 100 times or until the values change by less than .001. The result might not be exact, but inaccuracies this miniscule are not likely to cause concern.

3. Save all three worksheets one last time, and make certain no worksheets other than these are open before you move on.

Using Workbooks

If you work with several files simultaneously, as you did with the three worksheets you created in this chapter, you might find opening and saving the files separately to be a real chore. Even moving from one file to the next can be a hassle. To help you organize related Excel worksheets, macro sheets, and charts, Excel 4 introduces a new feature: workbooks. To give you a feel for what you can do with workbooks, let's create one now:

1. With the EMPLOYEE, ESTIMATE, and OVERHEAD worksheets still open, choose Save Workbook from the File menu. Excel displays the Save As dialog box.

Creating a workbook

2. Type *ratebook* as the workbook name, and click OK. Excel displays the workbook table of contents shown on the next page, listing all open worksheets.

Table of contents

Changing workbook elements

To add another file to a workbook, click the Add button in the workbook table of contents. Then either select the name of the file you want to add from the list that appears and click Add, or click New or Open to create a new document or locate an existing one. By default, added documents are bound into the workbook.

To remove a document from a workbook, highlight its name in the table of contents, and click the Remove button. Excel doesn't delete the file; it simply pulls the file out of the workbook as a separate file, which Excel then asks you to save when you save the workbook.

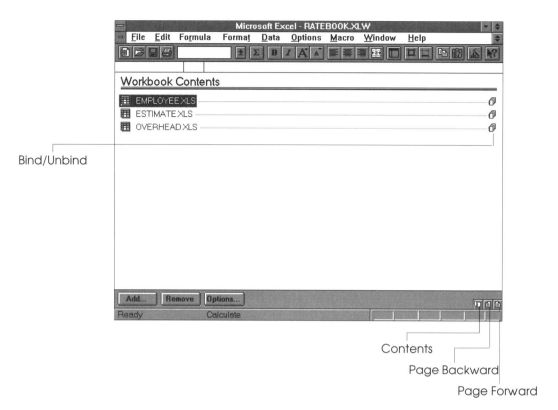

Bind/Unbind

Contents

Page Backward

Page Forward

Excel has consolidated copies of all three worksheets into the RATEBOOK.XLW workbook. The worksheet files are considered "bound" into the workbook, and you could now delete the three original files without losing any information. The three files are not linked in any way to the bound files, so if you do not delete the originals, they will not be updated when you make changes to the bound files.

Unbound workbook files

If you want to use a particular Excel worksheet or macro sheet in several workbooks, you can include it in each workbook as an "unbound" file so that it is still accessible to the other workbooks. Simply save it as part of the workbook, and then click the bind/unbind icon next to its name in the workbook table of contents. You can also highlight the filename, and click the Options button. In the Document Options dialog box, select the Separate File (Unbound) option, and then click OK. Each time you open the workbook, Excel opens the unbound file, and each time you save the workbook, Excel asks whether you want to save the unbound file as well. Because the unbound file exists separately on your hard disk, you cannot delete the original file as you can with bound files.

3. Page through the worksheets in the workbook by clicking the Page Forward and Page Backward buttons.

To open a specific file in the workbook, double-click its name in the table of contents, or bring up the shortcut menu for the table of contents by clicking—with the right mouse button—the Contents button in the bottom-right corner of the screen, and then choose the name of the file you want from the menu.

You now have a completed project estimate that takes into account your company's overhead costs as well as the direct costs associated with the project. As we said at the beginning of the chapter, you can adapt this set of worksheets in many ways to help you quickly assemble bids. You can also use the worksheets to compare the cost of doing projects in-house with estimates that you receive from vendors. And once you have set up a lookup table such as the employee-information table, you can link it to worksheets that perform a variety of other personnel-related calculations.

6

Excel Macros

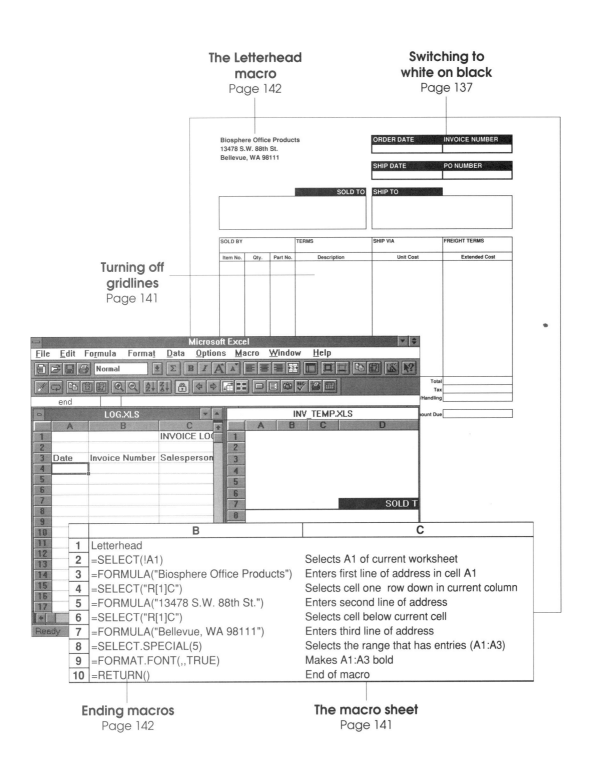

The Letterhead macro
Page 142

Switching to white on black
Page 137

Biosphere Office Products
13478 S.W. 88th St.
Bellevue, WA 98111

ORDER DATE   INVOICE NUMBER

SHIP DATE   PO NUMBER

SOLD TO   SHIP TO

| SOLD BY | TERMS | SHIP VIA | FREIGHT TERMS |
| Item No. | Qty. | Part No. | Description | Unit Cost | Extended Cost |

Turning off gridlines
Page 141

Microsoft Excel

File Edit Formula Format Data Options Macro Window Help

Normal

Total
Tax
/Handling
ount Due

end

LOG.XLS

	A	B	C
1			INVOICE LO
2			
3	Date	Invoice Number	Salesperson
4			
5			
6			
7			
8			
9			

INV_TEMP.XLS

SOLD T

Ready

	B	C
1	Letterhead	
2	=SELECT(!A1)	Selects A1 of current worksheet
3	=FORMULA("Biosphere Office Products")	Enters first line of address in cell A1
4	=SELECT("R[1]C")	Selects cell one row down in current column
5	=FORMULA("13478 S.W. 88th St.")	Enters second line of address
6	=SELECT("R[1]C")	Selects cell below current cell
7	=FORMULA("Bellevue, WA 98111")	Enters third line of address
8	=SELECT.SPECIAL(5)	Selects the range that has entries (A1:A3)
9	=FORMAT.FONT(,,TRUE)	Makes A1:A3 bold
10	=RETURN()	End of macro

Ending macros
Page 142

The macro sheet
Page 141

In this final chapter, we show you how to use the Excel macro feature, which can greatly increase your efficiency by automating some of the routine tasks associated with setting up worksheets. After you master the basics, even those of you whose palms get sweaty at the thought of having to deal with something as "techie" as a macro programming language will begin thinking of ways to put macros to use.

The example for this chapter is an invoice. In Chapter 3, we told you that we would show you a way to avoid having to manually input data into databases like invoice logs. The key to streamlining the data-input process is to generate forms such as invoices in Excel and then use a macro to make Excel do the work of transferring the data from the invoices to the invoice log.

Setting Up an Invoice

The invoice we are going to create in this chapter is shown on the previous page. Take a quick look to get oriented, and then let's get going.

1. Open a new worksheet, and save it as a template with the name INVOICE.XLT. (Recall that to save a worksheet in the template format, you select Template from the Save File As Type drop-down list box.)

2. Make the following entries in the indicated cells:

F1	ORDER DATE
G1	INVOICE NUMBER
F4	SHIP DATE
G4	PO NUMBER
D7	SOLD TO
F7	SHIP TO
A13	SOLD BY
D13	TERMS
F13	SHIP VIA
G13	FREIGHT TERMS
A15	Item No.
B15	Qty.
C15	Part No.
D15	Description
F15	Unit Cost

G15	Extended Cost
F30	Total
F31	Tax
F32	Shipping/Handling
F34	Amount Due

Now we'll do some formatting. We won't spell out every last detail, because by now you should have a good idea of how to track down commands and handle their dialog boxes.

1. Adjust the column widths as follows:

A, B, C	6.57
D, F, G	20
E	1

2. Use the Bold tool on the Standard toolbar to make all the cell entries bold.

3. Select F1, G1, F4, G4, D7, and F7, use the Patterns command to apply a black pattern to the cells, and then use the Font command to change the color of the text to white so that it stands out against the black background.

Switching to white on black

4. Select F1:F2, G1:G2, F4:F5, and G4:G5, and use the Border command to outline the cells with a thick border.

5. Use the alignment tools on the toolbar to center the entries in row 15 and right align the entries in D7 and F30:F34.

6. Select the following ranges, and use the Font command to reduce the size of the text to 8 points.

F2:G2	A8:D11
F5:G5	F8:G11
A13:G34	

7. Because you will be entering dates in two of the boxes at the top of the screen, let's format those cells now. Select F2 and F5. Then choose Number from the Format menu, and select the m/d/yy format from the Number Format dialog box.

8. Format the cells in the Unit Cost and Extended Cost columns as dollars and cents by selecting them and then selecting Currency from the Style drop-down list box.

With that out of the way, let's take a look at macros.

Creating Macros

An Excel macro is a set of instructions. When you run a macro, Excel moves sequentially through the instructions, doing whatever it is told to do. The instructions are written on a macro sheet that resembles a worksheet, in a form similar to the functions you enter in the formula bar. For example, this macro function

=SELECT(!C5)

tells Excel to select cell C5 on the active worksheet. (If you don't include the !, Excel selects C5 on the macro sheet.)

The macro recorder

To make it easy for new users to create macros right away, Excel has a macro recorder that you can use to record a series of keystrokes and commands as a macro. Excel takes care of translating the keystrokes and commands into the macro language and writing them on the macro sheet. You assign the macro a name so that you can "play it back" by opening the macro sheet, choosing Run from the Macro menu, and selecting the macro's name in the Run dialog box. You can also designate a shortcut key combination that you can press to run the macro. You can even link the macro to a "button" that you have created on the worksheet using one of Excel's graphics tools; clicking the button runs the macro.

Our discussion of macros will be necessarily brief and is not intended to make you an instant Excel macro expert. The idea is to get you thinking about whether tasks you perform routinely could be more efficiently carried out with macros, and to give you enough information to explore the topic further on your own. We start by showing you how to record a macro. Next, we take a look at macro sheets and the process by which you create macros from scratch. Then we assign a macro to a button. Finally, we examine a macro that transfers information from a filled-out invoice to an invoice log.

Recording Macros

To resemble the invoice at the beginning of the chapter, the invoice now on your screen needs borders around several ranges. You could use the Outline Border tool on the toolbar for this purpose, but that tool puts a thin border around ranges.

To create a thicker border, you must choose Border from the Format menu, select a line thickness, select Outline, and click OK. This set of steps is an ideal candidate for a simple recorded macro, so let's get to work.

1. Select A8:D11, the first range you want to outline.

2. Turn on the macro recorder by choosing Record from the Macro menu. Excel displays this dialog box:

The Outline macro

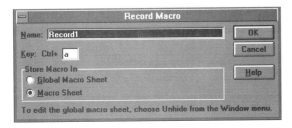

3. Type *Outline* as the name of the macro, and press Tab to move to the Key text box.

4. To be able to run the macro simply by pressing Ctrl-o, type *o* in the Key text box. Then click OK. Excel opens a macro sheet behind the current worksheet and begins recording. From now until you turn off the recorder, Excel will record every action you take.

5. Choose Border from the Format menu, select the second thickest line, select Outline, and click OK.

6. Choose Stop Recorder from the Macro menu to stop recording.

   While creating the macro, we outlined the selected range. Now let's use the Outline macro to format the next range:

1. Select F8:G11.

2. Choose Run from the Macro menu to display this dialog box:

The Run command

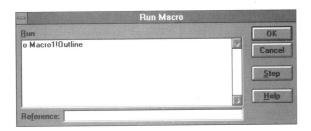

The *o* that precedes the macro name indicates the key you press with the Ctrl key to activate the macro.

3. Select Macro1!Outline, and click OK. Excel places a border around the range.

Now let's use the shortcut key combination to outline some additional ranges:

The shortcut key combination → 1. Select the following cells and ranges, pressing Ctrl-o after each selection:

A13:C14
A15
A16:A29
B16:B29
C15
C16:C29
D13:E14
D16:E29
F13:F14
F15
F16:F29
G13:G14
G15
G16:G29
G30
G31
G32
G34

Correct syntax

If you don't enter a function in a macro sheet (see page 143) with perfect syntax, Excel displays an error message and highlights the offending section of the function in the formula bar. Refer to the *Microsoft Excel Function Reference* for the correct macro function syntax.

Smart recorder

If you cancel an action, or click Cancel in a dialog box while Excel is recording a macro, the action is not recorded. If you Undo an action, Excel records both the action and the Undo command.

Halting macros

You can halt a running macro's progress at any point by simply clicking the Esc button. Excel displays a dialog box telling you at what cell it stopped the macro. You can then proceed by clicking the Halt, Step, Continue, or Goto buttons.

2. To make the borders stand out, turn off the worksheet's ←
gridlines by choosing Display from the Options menu,
deselecting Gridlines, and clicking OK. Here's the result:

Turning off gridlines

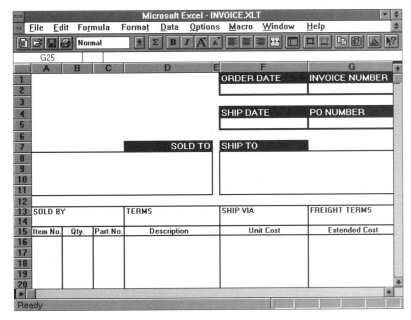

3. Now would be a good time to save the template again, to
preserve the work you have done so far.

Defining Macros from Scratch

You've probably noticed the blank hole in the top-left corner
of the invoice. Let's create a simple macro that will insert a
company name and address in this area. In the process, we'll
take a look at a macro sheet and learn something about the
Excel macro language. Follow these steps:

1. Choose Macro1 from the Window menu. Excel displays this ←
macro sheet:

The macro sheet

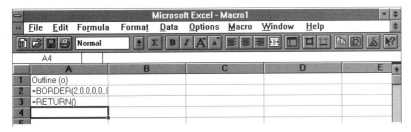

2. Widen column A so that you can see the whole macro.

Excel created the Macro1 macro sheet and wrote the macro instructions in column A when you recorded the Outline macro. The name of the macro, followed by the shortcut key you assigned, is located in cell A1. The BORDER macro function that creates the range outline is in cell A2. This function has six numeric arguments, each representing one of the options in the Border dialog box. So the function

=BORDER(2,0,0,0,0,,0)

selects a medium-thick outline for the border and leaves all the other options deselected.

Ending macros

The last function in the macro, =RETURN(), ends the macro. Macros that don't end with RETURN()—or alternatively HALT()—produce error messages.

A thorough examination of Excel's macro functions is beyond the scope of this book. Suffice it to say that an Excel macro function probably exists for every common worksheet task—and for many uncommon ones, too! You can consult the *Microsoft Excel Function Reference* for a complete listing of all the macro functions and their arguments. In the meantime, let's combine a few functions to create another macro.

1. Save Macro1 with the Save As command, assigning it the name GENERAL (for *general-purpose*.) Excel appends the extension XLM.

The Letterhead macro

2. In B1 of the macro sheet, type *Letterhead*, the macro's name.

Importing graphics

To create a really fancy letterhead, you can import a graphic into Excel from any application that supports the METAFILE file format. For example, you can create a logo in Paintbrush and paste it into a worksheet, like this: First, switch to Program Manager, and start Paintbrush. Create a small, simple graphic to use as a logo. Use the text tool to add the name and address. Then select the graphic, and copy it. Close Paintbrush, and return to Excel. Paste the graphic into the active worksheet. The graphic appears, surrounded by a set of handles that you can use to resize the graphic. Finally, click anywhere in the graphic, and drag it to the desired position on the worksheet.

By default, graphics in Excel move with the cells that are under them if you insert or delete other cells. Although the cells are hidden by the graphic, they can still contain text or numbers and can be used in calculations. Worksheet graphics can also function as macro buttons (see page 144 for more information).

3. To enter the company name and address, type the following macro functions in the indicated cells, exactly as you see them here. (You can substitute your own company's name and address if you want.) You don't have to type the comments in column C, which explain the action of each function.

	B	C
1	Letterhead	
2	=SELECT(!A1)	Selects A1 of current worksheet
3	=FORMULA("Biosphere Office Products")	Enters first line of address in cell A1
4	=SELECT("R[1]C")	Selects cell one row down in current column
5	=FORMULA("13478 S.W. 88th St.")	Enters second line of address
6	=SELECT("R[1]C")	Selects cell below current cell
7	=FORMULA("Bellevue, WA 98111")	Enters third line of address
8	=SELECT.SPECIAL(5)	Selects the range that has entries (A1:A3)
9	=FORMAT.FONT(,,TRUE)	Makes A1:A3 bold
10	=RETURN()	End of macro

4. Select cell B2, and choose Define Name from the Formula menu to display this dialog box:

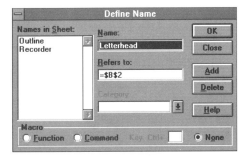

5. Excel suggests the name Letterhead, which is just what we want. Click the Command button, and then type the letter *l* in the Ctrl+ text box. Finally, click OK.

Now let's test the new macro:

1. Choose the INVOICE.XLT template file from the Window menu, and select cell A1.

2. Press Ctrl-l to run the macro. Here's the result:

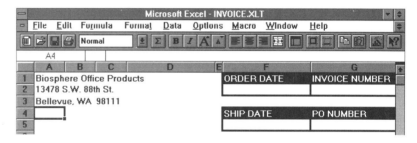

Congratulations. You've just written your first macro.

Assigning Macros to Buttons

As we mentioned earlier, you can assign a macro to a button on the worksheet and then run the macro simply by clicking the button. You create the button using the Button tool on the Utility toolbar, or one of the graphics tools on the Drawing toolbar. Both are shown at the top of the next page.

Object Linking and Embedding (OLE)

Excel supports object linking and embedding, or OLE. OLE goes several steps beyond simple cutting and pasting to create a conduit between a source and a destination document. You can use OLE to exhange data between Excel documents, or between an Excel document and an external document. Both source and destination applications must support OLE.

Although the terms *linking* and *embedding* are used together, they are really quite different. Linking allows some programs to automatically update pasted data. For example, you can paste an Excel worksheet into a Word for Windows document in such a way that, whenever you change the worksheet data, the Word document is updated correspondingly. Embedding is used to paste an object that doesn't necessarily need to be updated, but that you might need to change at a later date in the originating program. For example, if you embed a Paintbrush graphic in an Excel document and need to change some aspect of the graphic, you can double-click the embedded bitmap image to open a Paintbrush window within Excel and make the changes. You must have enough memory to run both programs at the same time. Use the Insert Object command on Excel's Edit menu to display a list of programs from which you can embed objects. Commands for linking and embedding are not identical in all programs that support it, but they always appear in the Edit menu as some variation of Paste Special or Insert Object.

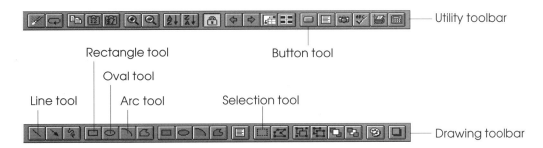

Line tool   Arc tool   Selection tool

Rectangle tool   Button tool

Oval tool

— Utility toolbar

— Drawing toolbar

Buttons are useful tools because they provide instant access to macros and because they serve as a graphic reminder of the macros' availability.

To see how buttons work, try this:

1. Display the Utility toolbar by using the toolbar shortcut menu or the Toolbars dialog box.

2. Clear the address from cells A1:A3 of INVOICE.XLT, and click the Button tool. The pointer changes to a cross hair.

Creating buttons

3. Drag the cross-hair pointer to draw a marquee that roughly covers cells A6:C7. Excel creates a button and displays this dialog box:

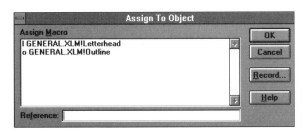

4. The Assign Macro list box lists the macros available in open macro sheets. Select Letterhead, and click OK.

5. With the button selected, highlight the Button 1 label, and type *Address*. (If necessary, select the button again by pressing Ctrl while clicking it.)

6. Click elsewhere on the worksheet to deselect the button. Then click the button to run the Letterhead macro. The result is shown on the next page.

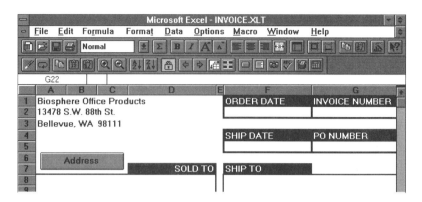

Deleting buttons

7. Use the Selection tool on the Drawing toolbar to delete the button, delete the text in cells A1:A3, and then save and close INVOICE.XLT.

Logging Invoice Data with a Macro

You now know enough about macros to follow along as we create one that will take the information you enter in a copy of INVOICE.XLT and record it in an invoice log. This macro can be adapted for many uses. For example, you could use the techniques you learned while creating the invoice to develop a contacts template. You could then adapt the macro to pull information about each new client you work with into a name and address database. Or you might want to create an expense-report template and adapt the macro to record expenses in a reimbursement summary.

Adapting macros

Macro button changes

If you need to assign another macro to the button or you want to change the button name or size, use the Selection tool to select it, or hold down the Ctrl key and click the button. Then choose Assign to Object from the Macro menu, and select another macro.

Graphic macro buttons

As we've said, you can assign macros to any graphic object you create, even a line or a text box. Just select the object or group of objects, and choose Assign To Object from the Macro menu. Excel displays the Assign To Object dialog box. Simply select a macro, and click OK. The next time you click the object, the macro runs.

Before we can work on the macro, we need to create the invoice-log worksheet, so let's get moving.

Setting Up the Invoice Log

For demonstration purposes, we'll keep this log very simple. Follow these steps:

1. Open a new worksheet, and make the following entries in the indicated cells:

C1	INVOICE LOG
A3	Date
B3	Invoice Number
C3	Salesperson
D3	Amount of Sale

2. Select A1:D3, and click the Bold tool.

3. Format column A with a date format, and format column D with the Currency style.

4. Adjust the column widths so that you can see all the entries, and make the Date column a bit wider.

5. We want Excel to append new invoices to the end of the invoice log, so select cell A4, choose the Define Name command from the Formula menu, type *end*, and click OK.

   <- Designating the end of a database

6. Save the worksheet with the name LOG.XLS, leaving it open on your screen.

   That's it for the log. Now let's move on to create the macro.

Creating the Log Macro

The Log macro we are going to create is a relatively straightforward combination of Copy and Paste commands. Take a little time as you enter the functions to figure out what each one does.

1. Choose New from the File menu, select Macro Sheet, and click OK. Save the new macro sheet as LOG.XLM.

   <- The Log macro

2. Enter the functions shown on the next page exactly as you see them. (You can copy and paste A5:A9 three times and edit the copies, rather than typing all the entries from scratch.) Again, you don't have to type the comments in column B.

	A	B
1	Log	
2	=FORMULA.GOTO("LOG.XLS!end")	Activates cell named "end" in invoice log
3	=INSERT(3)	Inserts a new row above selected cell
4	=FORMULA.GOTO("INV_TEMP.XLS!R2C6")	Selects order date in invoice
5	=COPY()	Copies it
6	=FORMULA.GOTO("LOG.XLS!end")	Activates cell named "end" in invoice log
7	=SELECT("R(-1)C1")	Selects column 1 of row above "end"
8	=PASTE.SPECIAL(3,1,FALSE,FALSE)	Pastes order date without formatting
9	=FORMULA.GOTO("INV_TEMP.XLS!R2C7")	Selects invoice number
10	=COPY()	Copies it
11	=ACTIVATE("LOG.XLS")	Activates invoice log
12	=SELECT("RC2")	Selects column 2 of current row
13	=PASTE.SPECIAL(3,1,FALSE,FALSE)	Pastes invoice number without formatting
14	=FORMULA.GOTO("INV_TEMP.XLS!R14C1")	Selects salesperson's name
15	=COPY()	Copies it
16	=ACTIVATE("LOG.XLS")	Activates invoice log
17	=SELECT("RC3")	Selects column 3 of current row
18	=PASTE.SPECIAL(3,1,FALSE,FALSE)	Pastes salesperson's name without format
19	=FORMULA.GOTO("INV_TEMP.XLS!R34C7")	Selects amount of sale
20	=COPY()	Copies it
21	=ACTIVATE("LOG.XLS")	Activates invoice log
22	=SELECT("RC4")	Selects column 4 of current row
23	=PASTE.SPECIAL(3,1,FALSE,FALSE)	Pastes amount of sale without formatting
24	=RETURN()	End of macro

3. Select cell A2, and choose the Define Name command from the Formula menu. Accept the default name, Log, click the Command button, and then click OK.

4. Save the macro sheet again.

R1C1 notation

The R1C1 cell referencing scheme references cells by their row and column position in relation to the active cell. The easiest way to understand this notation is with a few examples. If the active cell is B2, RC is the cell in the same row and the same column as the active cell—in other words, it is cell B2, the active cell itself. R[–1]C is the cell in the row above and the same column as the active cell—in other words, it is cell B1. R[–1]C[–1] is the cell in the row above and one column to the left—in other words, it is cell A1. Similarly, R[1]C[1] is the cell in the row below and one column to the right—cell C3.

User-defined macros

By default, Excel puts any user-defined macros under the User Defined category in the Paste Functions dialog box. However, you can save your macros in a different category by selecting the category you want in the Define Name dialog box.

Running the Macro

Now for the acid test. We'll open an invoice, make a few entries, and then run the macro. Here goes:

1. Open a copy of INVOICE.XLT. The Log macro expects the invoice from which it is to transfer information to be called INV_TEMP.XLS, so save the invoice with that name.

2. Enter a date in cell F2, a number in cell G2, a name in cell A14, and a dollar amount in cell G34.

3. Choose LOG.XLS from the Window menu, and then resize LOG.XLS and INV_TEMP.XLS, like this:

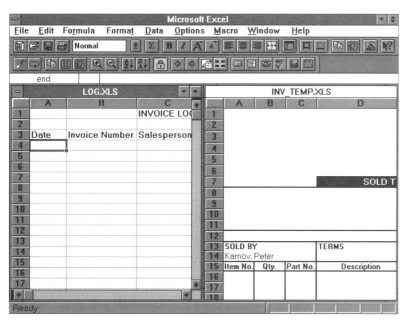

4. Choose Run from the Macro menu, select Log, and click OK. If you have entered the macro correctly, Excel transfers the information you entered to the log.

5. Activate the invoice and save it with a new name—the invoice number would be a good choice, as long as it has no more than eight characters.

   You might want to open another copy of INVOICE.XLT, make a few entries, and run the macro, to see how Excel appends the information from successive invoices to the invoice log.

Dialog Editor

Excel ships with a program called Dialog Editor, with which you can create custom dialog boxes for use in macros. After you create the basic dialog box structure, you paste it into a macro sheet, where it is translated into a set of macro-language instructions. You then tie these instructions to specific tasks in Excel. (See the Excel documentation for more information.)

If the Macro Doesn't Work

Macro error messages

If Excel encounters an error in the macro, it stops and displays a message announcing the location of the error. You can then click the Goto button to go directly to the cell on the macro sheet that caused the error. The most likely cause of errors is typos. But if you can't see anything wrong with the offending function, Excel offers another way to sleuth out the cause of the problem.

Stepping through a macro

In the Macro Error and the Macro Run dialog boxes is a Step option that allows you to step through the macro a function at a time. Clicking the Step button displays a small window, like this one:

Excel displays the first macro function and its location so that you can examine it. If you click the Step Into button, Excel executes the displayed function and displays the next function. You thus have the opportunity to see the macro in slow motion and have a better chance of spotting errors.

Well, that quick overview of macros winds up the book. You are now equipped with the tools you need to create some pretty sophisticated worksheets and should be familiar enough with Excel to explore on your own.

Index

About the Authors

Joyce Cox
Before cofounding Online Press, Cox was Managing Editor of Microsoft Press. She is coauthor of five *Quick Course*™ titles.

Patrick Kervran
Coauthor of *A Quick Course in Windows 3.1* and *A Quick Course in Lotus 1-2-3 for Windows*, Kervran lives in Seattle, WA.

Other *Quick Course*™ Books

Don't miss the other titles in our *Quick Course*™ series! Quality books at the unbeatable price of $12.95.

A Quick Course in Windows 3.1   ISBN 1-879399-14-8
A Quick Course in Word 2.0 for Windows   ISBN 1-879399-05-9
A Quick Course in Lotus 1-2-3 for Windows   ISBN 1-879399-07-5
A Quick Course in WordPerfect for Windows   ISBN 1-879399-06-7
A Quick Course in DOS 5   ISBN 1-879399-03-2
A Quick Course in WordPerfect 5.1   ISBN 1-879399-01-6
A Quick Course in Paradox for Windows   ISBN 1-879399-12-1 (Summer 1992)
A Quick Course in Lotus 1-2-3 Release 2.4   ISBN 1-879399-18-0 (Summer 1992)

Plus more to come...

For a copy of our latest catalog, call us at (206) 641-3434 or write to us at:

Online Press Inc.
14320 NE 21st Street, Suite 18
Bellevue, WA 98007

Quick Course™ books are distributed to bookstores in the U.S. by *Publishers Group West*, Emeryville, CA (510-658-3453 or 800-788-3123) and by *major wholesalers*; in Australia by *Step Up Systems* (03-427-0168); and in the United Kingdom by *Computer Bookshops Ltd.* (021-706-1188).